# Nostos

## Volume II, Number 2
## 2018

Lawrence Tjernell, Editor

For more information, go to www.longshippress.com. The individual poems, short stories, and art of this edition have been copyrighted by their authors. Inquiries about individual works or writers may be directed to
Lawrence Tjernell, Editor
Longship Press (info@longshippress.com).

ISBN-10:
0-578-42769-0

ISBN-13:
978-0-578-42769-0

L O N G S H I P    P R E S S

Printed in the United States

Longship Press 1122 4th Street San Rafael, California 94901

*For*
*Albert, Beda, Josephus, Francis,*
*Sture, and Eveline*

# Acknowledgments and Appreciations

Some of the poems in this edition of Nostos are reprinted. I would like to acknowledge gratefully the following publications and authors.

Rebecca Foust: "Mom's Canoe," *Atlanta Review*, 2007. "Ice Skating at Night," *The Hudson Review*, 2011. "No Longer Medusa," *Mudfish*, 2008.

Louise Glück: The seven "Telemachus" poems and the poem "Reunion," all from *Meadowlands*. Copyright © 1996 by Louise Glück. Reprinted by permission of HarperCollins Publishers.

Karen Poppy: "On Your Birthday," *Sky Island Journal*, Issue 5, Summer 2018.

James Tipton: "Jettisoned," *Blue Unicorn*, 2017.

Javier Zamora, "Postpartum" and "Then, It Was So" from *Unaccompanied*. Copyright © 2017 by Javier Zamora. Reprinted with the permission of The Permissions Company, Inc., on behalf of Copper Canyon Press.

I want to thank Meryl Natchez for having alerted fine writers to the call for submissions for this edition. Additionally, I want to thank Javier Zamora for allowing us to reprint two poems from his remarkable collection "Unaccompanied," and to express my gratitude to Rebecca Foust for helping make all that possible.

This issue of *Nostos* is the "familial" issue, a collection of poetry, short fiction, and art concerned with the realationships between and among mother/father/daughter/son. We are especially pleased to reprint eight poems by Louise Glück. From her collection *Meadowlands*, we have the seven "Telemechus" poems and the poem "Reunion," a tender culmination.

And my ever-present appreciation of my Swedish and English/Irish grandparents, and my brave and sustaining parents.

— Ed.

# Table of Contents

# Foreword

I first encountered Louise Glück's poems as a grad student at Warren Wilson when a professor assigned them as an antidote to my own overly-decorated work. I read *The House on Marshland*, *Wild Iris*, *Averno*, and *Ararat* all in one glorious week, loving Glück's use of myth and fairy tale and excited by her spare and unapologetically acerbic style. What really intoxicated me, though, was her subject. My previous reading had encouraged me to think of marriage and family as "women's topics," and somehow therefore lesser subjects in literature. The notion that family is not only a legitimate but in fact a noble and worthwhile subject — one that offers tremendous opportunity to explore issues of broader humanity — was a breakthrough for my own writing. The poems by Louise Glück in this issue of *Nostos* are from *Meadowlands*, a collection that looks at *The Odyssey* in a new way, embodying Penelope and Odysseus in a contemporary marriage conversation resonant with the domestic minutiae and bickering that can overlay fundamental and tragic conflict. A myth is a story everybody already knows and maybe has always known, and putting contemporary vernacular in the mouths of mythic characters allows Glück to show that her themes of love, grief, and loss are timeless and universal.

Multiple voices speak in *Meadowlands*, spinning narratives that weave a rich tapestry of perspectives. In its forty-seven poems are at least four distinct sequences belonging to Penelope, Odysseus, Circe, and Telemachus, whose sequence is presented here. The poems are mordantly funny, social, bitter, judgmental, and sometimes unexpectedly merciful. Within the "inflexible templates" of myth, Glück's characters become "fully, elastically human," so much so that "her Dido sounds like Glück, her Penelope sounds like Glück, her Persephone sounds like Glück; even the bad guys in these stories get to talk, and, when they do, they sound — surprise — a lot like Glück." ["The Body Artist: *Louise Glück's collected poems*," by Dan Chiasson, *The New Yorker*, 11/12/12.]

Some may view Glück's distinctive stamp on her voice-throwing as autobiographical (or, horrors, "confessional"), but I prefer to think of it as what we call "poetic voice," with each persona embodying — as in Shakespeare — some essential aspect of the human drama. In her book *Proofs and Theories: Essays on Poetry* (Ecco 1995), Glück writes that testimony in poetry is not the recounting of circumstances but their *transcription*. As in gene expression, the process of transcription involves more than mere copying; it involves the creation of something new. The source of art is experience; the end product, truth. It is the job of the artist to survey the facts and then to manipulate them — even (as Picasso famously said) sometimes to "lie" — all in the service of that end. In *Meadowlands*, truth is offered from various perspectives in one representative family, and the reader, as one who overhears all the conversations and monologues, ultimately is called to bear witness.

Telemachus is the son of Penelope and Odysseus whose marriage is faltering, and the tone in his poems ranges from lyrical to outrageously comic, with the same dark biting humor, depressive realism, grief, and detachment seen in Glück's other poems. We are fortunate to have Glück's own words about the Telemachus poems and how they came to be included in *Meadowlands*:

> What the book ended up . . . being was a double narrative, in which the dissolution of a contemporary marriage . . . elaborated in a series of petulant, comic conversations and private bickerings, [that] alternates with, is threaded through, with the story of Odysseus and Penelope. And the last thing that was added to the manuscript was a group of poems. Let me backtrack and say that it was clear to me for a very long time that though I thought I had done everything I knew how to do, the book was not finished. It was clear that it was not done. And when something is a single undertaking, as was this book, if it isn't done, it's a failure. It's like a novel that hasn't worked out. It isn't that you have ten poems instead of twenty, you have nothing. And I kept thinking, well what's missing is a sort of somberness, maybe, or a deep sorrow

that should be running through this. I had shown the manuscript, in part, to a friend of mine who's a classicist, and . . . she said, "Well, you have no Telemachus"… And I thought, well, why don't I try Telemachus. ["In the Magnificent Region of Courage: An Interview with Louise Glück," by Grace Cavalieri, *Beltway Poetry Quarterly*, Vol. 7, No. 4 (2006)]

Asked whether Telemachus is the major figure in *Meadowlands*, Glück says:

I love this little boy. He saved my book, and the poems in his voice were written very, very, very quickly, over a period of about ten days or two weeks, in busses, and in guest room beds, and elevators. Once I had the sound of his voice, which is to say the sound of his mind, I knew how to finish my book, and I did the poems in an exultant rush … [Id.]

How wonderful to have these poems before us again in the entirety and purity of their extracted sequence, in this issue of *Nostos*! My thanks goes to editor Lawrence Tjernell for his tireless efforts to create and edit this wonderful new journal, especially this issue devoted to the timeless, universal and yes — noble — subject of family in literature.


~ Rebecca Foust

# Louise Glück

Louise Glück's collection *The Wild Iris* won the Pulitzer Prize for Poetry in 1993. The author of twelve books of poetry, she has received the National Book Critics Circle Award for Poetry, the William Carlos Williams Award, and the PEN/Martha Albrand Award for Nonfiction. She served as the U.S. Poet Laureate (2003-2004). Her collection *Faithful and Virtuous Night* (2014) won the National Book Award for Poetry. Louise Glück teaches at Yale University and lives in Cambridge, Massachusetts.

# Telemachus' Detachment

When I was a child looking
at my parents' lives, you know
what I thought? I thought
heartbreaking. Now I think
heartbreaking, but also
insane. Also
very funny.

# Telemachus' Guilt

Patience of the sort my mother
practiced on my father
(which in his self–
absorption he mistook
for tribute though it was in fact
a species of rage — didn't he
ever wonder why he was
so blocked in expressing
his native abandon?): it infected
my childhood. Patiently
she fed me; patiently
she supervised the kindly
slaves who attended me, regardless
of my behavior, an assumption
I tested with increasing
violence. It seemed clear to me
that from her perspective
I didn't exist, since
my actions had
no power to disturb her: I was
the envy of my playmates.
In the decades that followed
I was proud of my father
for staying away
even if he stayed away for
the wrong reasons;

I used to smile
when my mother wept.
I hope now she could
forgive that cruelty; I hope
she understood how like
her own coldness it was,
a means of remaining
separate from what
one loves deeply.

# Telemachus' Kindness

When I was younger I felt
sorry for myself
compulsively; in practical terms,
I had no father; my mother
lived at her loom hypothesizing
her husband's erotic life; gradually
I realized no child on that island had
a different story; my trials
were the general rule, common
to all of us, a bond
among us, therefore
with humanity: what
a life my mother had, without
compassion for my father's
suffering, for a soul
ardent by nature, thus
ravaged by choice, nor had my father
any sense of her courage, subtly
expressed as inaction, being
himself prone to dramatizing,
to acting out: I found
I could share these perceptions
with my closest friends, as they shared
theirs with me, to test them,
to refine them: as a grown man
I can look at my parents
impartially and pity them both: I hope
always to be able to pity them.

# Telemachus' Dilemma

I can never decide
what to write on
my parents' tomb. I know
what he wants: he wants
*beloved*, which is
certainly to the point, particularly
if we count all
the women. But
that leaves my mother
out in the cold. She tells me
this doesn't matter to her
in the least; she prefers
to be represented by
her own achievement. It seems
tactless to remind them
that one does not
honor the dead by perpetuating
their vanities, their
projections of themselves.
My own taste dictates
accuracy without
garrulousness; they are
my parents, consequently
I see them together,
sometimes inclining to
*husband and wife*, other times
to *opposing forces*.

# Telemachus' Fantasy

Sometimes I wonder about my father's
years on those islands: why
was he so attractive
to women? He was in straits then, I suppose
desperate. I believe
women like to see a man
still whole, still standing, but
about to go to pieces: such
disintegration reminds them
of passion. I think of them as living
their whole lives
completely undressed. It must have
dazzled him, I think, women
so much younger than he was
evidently wild for him, ready
to do anything he wished. Is it
fortunate to encounter circumstances
so responsive to one's own will, to live
so many years
unquestioned, unthwarted? One
would have to believe oneself
entirely good or worthy. I
suppose in time either
one becomes a monster or
the beloved sees what one is. I never
wish for my father's life

nor have I any idea
what he sacrificed
to survive that moment. Less dangerous
to believe he was drawn to them
and so stayed
to see who they were. I think, though,
as an imaginative man
to some extent he
became who they were.

# Telemachus' Confession

They
were not better off
when he left; ultimately
I was better off. This
amazed me, not because I was convinced
I needed them both but because
long into adulthood I retained
something of the child's
hunger for ritual. How else address
that sense of being
insufficiently loved? Possibly
all children are
insufficiently loved; I
wouldn't know. But all along
they each wanted something
different from me: having
to fabricate the being
each required in any
given moment was
less draining than
having to be
two people. And after awhile
I realized I *was*
actually a person; I had

my own voice, my own perceptions, though
I came to them late. I no longer regret
the terrible moment in the fields,
the ploy that took
my father away. My mother
grieves enough for us all.

# Telemachus' Burden

Nothing
was exactly difficult because
routines develop, compensations
for perceived
absences and omissions. My mother
was the sort of woman
who let you know she was suffering and then
denied that suffering since in her view
suffering was what slaves did; when
I tried to console her,
to relieve her misery, she
rejected me. I now realize
if she'd been capable of honesty
she would have been
a Stoic. Unfortunately
she was a queen, she wanted it understood
at every moment she had chosen
her own destiny. She would have had to be
insane to choose that destiny. Well,
good luck to my father, in my opinion
a stupid man if he expects
his return to diminish
her isolation; perhaps
he came back for that.

# Reunion

When Odysseus has returned at last
unrecognizable to Ithaca and killed
the suitors swarming the throne room,
very delicately he signals to Telemachus
to depart: as he stood twenty years ago,
he stands now before Penelope.
On the palace floor, wide bands of sunlight turning
from gold to red. He tells her
nothing of those years, choosing to speak instead
exclusively of small things, as would be
the habit of a man and woman long together:
once she sees who he is, she will know what he's done.
And as he speaks, ah,
tenderly he touches her forearm.

# Javier Zamora

Born in El Salvador, Javier Zamora published his first collection of poems, *Unaccompanied*, in 2017 (Copper Canyon Press). He is the recipient of the Lannan Literary Fellowship in Poetry (2017) and the Wallace Stegner Fellowship, Stanford University (2016-2018). Other fellowships include those from Colgate University, The Frost Pace, The Macondo Writers Workshop, and the National Endowment for the Arts Literature Fellowship. He is the cofounder of "Undocupoets," an advocacy group calling on publishers to extend grants and first-book contest awards to writers with DACA status or Temporary Protected Status.

# Then, It Was So

To tell you I was leaving
I waited and waited
rethinking first sentences in my sleep,
I didn't sleep,
and my heart was a watermelon
split each night. Outside,
3 a.m. was the same as bats
and you were our kerosene lamp.

Amor, I thought it was something
we were in that day, hiding
from bullets in sugarcane, my chest
pressed against the gossamers
stuck to your thighs,
when stars swam inside you.

The last second has passed
and I can't forget one centimeter.
To kiss each cheek,
your lips, your forehead.
I miss our son. I miss the faint wick
on his skin. How I held him
and how I wanted to then, though
I didn't wake him.

That dawn, I needed to say
you remind me of my father
and leaving is a bucket of mosquitoes
no one empties. Cariño,
it was so quiet when I started
counting the days
I wasn't woken by him.

                    – Dad, age 19

# Postpartum

My son's in the other room. This little
burlap sack of rice came out yellow,
some deficiency, got incubated, hasn't
stopped crying — his father wasn't there,
he was "out fishing." His father's mother came
next day saying, I'm saint I'm saint,
I won't let you trick him. "The big saint"
wanted to check my son for birthmarks
to see if he's really Zamora. She found them
near his balls. Esa puta didn't even give
enough for powered milk. And don't
tell me he looks like his father, maybe
the back of his hair. I know his father
doesn't love me. You don't have to tell me:
you're stupid, you're jealous, crazy.
Maybe he hears, I wish he hears my moans
when he's on top of his whores.
Like I don't know. I am crazy, but not
estúpida. If I catch him, me las va pagar.
Me las va pagar, that dipshit
deep in debt over a fishing boat
he can't catch nothing in. My son
won't drink from me. I pump breasts,
rub sugar and honey on them,
¿why won't he drink from me?

— Mom, age 18

# Rebecca Foust

Rebecca Foust's books include *Paradise Drive* (2015 Press 53 Award for Poetry), reviewed in the *Times Literary Supplement*, *The San Francisco Chronicle,* and the *Georgia, Harvard,* and *Hudson Reviews.* Recent recognitions include the Cavafy Prize, the James Hearst Poetry Prize, the Lascaux Prize for Flash Fiction, the *American Literary Review* Fiction Prize, the Constance Rooke Creative Nonfiction Prize, and fellowships from Hedgebrook, MacDowell, Sewanee, and The Frost Place. Foust is Poet Laureate of Marin County, Poetry Editor for Women's Voices for Change, and an Assistant Editor and Team Leader reading fiction for *Narrative Magazine.*

# Mom's Canoe

Do you remember your old canoe?
Wooden wide-bellied, tapered ends
made to slip through tight river bends
swiftly, like shadow.
Hull ribbed delicately, wing of bird,
skimming the water more glider than boat,
ponderous in portage, weightless afloat.
Frail origami, vessel of air,
wide shallow saucer suspended where
shallows met shadows near the old dam.
Remember how it glowed like honey in summer
rubbed with beeswax and turpentine
against leaks, cracks, weather and time.
All your housekeeping went into that canoe,
then you floated high, bow lifted,
arced up like flight, all magic, power,
evening light. You j-stroking,
side-slipping, eddying out, frugal
with movement, all without effort,
just like you walked and ran.
I still see you rising from water to sky,
paddle held high,
river drops limning its edge.
Brown diamonds catch the light as you lift, then dip.
Parting the current, you slip
silently through the evening shadows.
You, birdsong, watersong, slanting light,
following river bend, swallowed from sight.

# No Longer Medusa

When I had you, daughter, I gave birth
to my mirror,
the chink in my armor.
Once, I turned men to adamantine
with a glance, dove from cliffs
into dark quarries, swung grapevines
over ravines, rode arcs of tall birch trees
into the ground. Now I am alive
all night with fear for you, undone
by your sweet, milky breath,
the bobcat tufts on your ears,
your pink ribbon gums.
You freeze my heart to stone
when I measure your foot with my thumb.

# Preparation for Pirouette

When my newborn lay gray, silent, and still,
I saw a notch in the skin at his collarbone — a petal
puckered by rain or, over an open mouth, a veil
of chiffon sucked in — breath's first pirouette.
When my mother lay dying, what pierced me
was not her mouth's black puckered O. It was not
her hands going slack at the rails, or even her eye
sunk into iris-less stone. It was that last breath
shirring the flesh at her throat, the sign that she
— drawn utterly inwardly taut — was braced
to her clenched core against death. One day, my turn
to make a wreath of my arms, rise up en pointe —

then, whip-pivot-spot — be gone.

Let my throat ache then, be notched. Each flawed dawn.

# Hangfire

You asked my permission
to shave your legs
just before you confessed
you'd done it that morning;
you made your first
double play at age eight
and memorized the periodic
table at nine. Your best use
for boys was to beat them
at anything. Ms. M. called you
"saucy" and Ms. G.,
a "pearl-handled pistol."
They made us laugh
and laughed with us,
but not the next teacher, a man
who, when you questioned
his blackboard error, wrote home
to complain that your mind
was "unduly" quick
then made it his mission
to dampen your spark.
The school named a new building
for him, and put his face
on the cover of its alumnae magazine,
how you learned what it means
to be smart, and a woman.

# Ice Skating at Night

### after Kafka

I push off and ride to
the center of the dark lake
then head for where
I know the river

feeds in, my blades tracing
moonlit Sanskrit
on the through-the-glass-
darkly daguerreotyped ice.

The way is away
from the voices
and bonfires, the way
is dark and more narrow

with trees bending down,
threading bootlaces
with branches to trip me
on the way to a place

known to only my dead
mother and me. I push
and pump until I find it,
the black, un-etched ice

doming a deep secret
spring. And now

something is coming apart,
the body forgetting

how firmly it once was
embodied, a lock set
in rebarred concrete
giving way to the moss's

invisible feast. The least river
succumbs first to spring,
and so I begin to breathe
in moonlight and smoke,

breathing out into where
the ice floe is breaking.
Ahead gleams a dark,
twisting ribbon of river,

behind brims a wide bowl
of skaters, laughter,
and warmth from the fire.
I set my sawtooth edge

to glide and swoop
like unchecked error,
the ice a hand mirror
holding me as well

as it holds my reflection.
I don't want anymore
to hide from myself
where I'm going — deep,

deep into some far
and alone recede where
my mother led me,
thirty years gone. If I keep on,

I know I will get there,
to the dark heart
at the heart of the heart
of this vast, frozen lake.

# fearsome & wondrous

the man slumped in his own piss
at the storefront    something about the face
the flutter of pulse at his jaw

something about the eyes
I recognize    I will try to speak again
of the treble trill

of the redwing blackbird
& sun gilding the window into a scrim
behind which it is possible

to think I see God    he died
for a moment when he was born    my son
who now stands a man

fearsomely & wondrously made
who intuits light as the last exhaled breath
of dying stars    who sees

the bent leaf in time to step
to the side    who walks without armor or mask
braced against every ion

all-at-once coming at him
on the earth's shifting plates    he sways
threading through trees

sometimes in bloom & sometimes
bare in the rain & somehow    he finds his way

Photo by Bobbe Besold

# Lisa Rappoport

Lisa Rappoport is a letterpress printer and book artist, creating artist's books and poetry broadsides under the imprint Littoral Press, as well as a book designer and poet. Her work is in national and international collections and has been included in such surveys as *500 Handmade Books* and *1000 Artists' Books*. She has two books of poetry: *Words Fail {Me}*, an artist's book commissioned by the San Francisco Center for the Book (2014), and *Aftermaths/Figments*, a chapbook from Etherdome (2009). Her poetry appeared most recently in the anthologies *The 2017 Richmond Anthology of Poetry* and *Pluto: New Horizons for a Lost Horizon* (North Atlantic Books, 2015), and the journals *Caesura* (2016) and *San Diego Poetry Annual* (2017-18). Her poetry collection, *Penumbra*, is forthcoming from Longship Press.

# Coffee Cake

*Cream 1/8 lb. butter, 1 cup sugar*
(or less if history's undertow tugs
you toward salt, toward bitterness).
*Add 2 whole eggs, 1 1/2 cups flour, sifted*
with powdery memories of your mother's kitchen,
entire, fragmented, smashed, a mishmash of love,
regret, cracked hope, nourishment bestowed
and withheld, acrid white dust. Leaven with
*1 1/2 tsp. baking powder,* for levity, even
chemically induced; for ease,
whatever is light, what rises, what floats.

What is a mother's recipe without
*milk, 3/4 cup,* life's beginning, always shadowed
by the nuance of turning, the possibility of souring.
*One tsp. vanilla or maple flavoring —*
the ersatz favored above the genuine: was that
to pinch pennies or because it lasted when the real
thing, what my parents thought real, didn't
persist, fermented perhaps, drunk on its own
sweetness? Can any pleasure, any promise,
endure? Better not to risk wrecking
on the shoals of what might not be sure.

Decades later, awash in my own hesitations,
I wonder: Why not blueberries? Fresh or frozen,
summer or winter, that untamed blue. The topping:

*Mix nuts, cinnamon, sugar, sprinkle well over batter* before *baking.*
To everything an order, a natural harmony, do this and that
must follow; keep safe by circumscribing
life. Can we stop death from taking
its turn?

My mother tells us what must be done:
*Bake 20-30 minutes in oblong pan at 350 degrees.*
That "oblong" catches my eye, the beauty
of the word in her slanted handwriting, the slight
unexpectedness of the choice among others more
expected, those elongated consonants, the second
"o" practically a diphthong, the feel of the sounds
in my mouth like our rounded ancestral Russian,
diasporal Yiddish, the syllables of Jews on the run
yet conversing, keeping the mother tongues
alive, streaming off ships to congregate
in the kitchens of the New World and partake
in the ritual breaking of the bread,
tasting the salt, the coffee, the cake.

# Arc

Hospital stays framed the two ends
of her married life. Her bulk was at its least
those times and climbed a bell curve of mass
in between. During her engagement she was
so happy she walked on air. Air failed her,
and she plummeted down the subway stairs
and lay six weeks in a white bed, to rise
slimmer than ever before and wed
my father. So thrilled, she said, to be
wanted, to find a man who would
have her. Convinced, then and forever,
that love lay beyond her horizon,
an undeserved gift, she was doomed
to lifelong gratitude, to visions
of love vanishing into thin air,
someone else's air. She didn't claim
what was hers; the shame of size muzzled
any unvoiced protests. At last cancer
stole her flesh and laid her
diminished body down on those white
sheets, in a room where my father
sat silent, mourning, still full as a stone
well of his unbelieved-in love.

# The Presence

Even now I get that feeling sometimes my mother
is near, just out of earshot, listening, and she
wants me to talk to her, though we never did
talk much; still, she knows what's going on,
as mothers know when you've done something
you shouldn't, or haven't done something you should,
and I want to talk to her now, but it's too late.
You didn't speak of her after her death,
I was alone in my grief, my complicated
sorrow, my remorse and relief and regrets.
For you it was over, and why not, you'd never
met; now you never would. Yet she welcomed you
into the family, such as it was, she looked
forward to meeting you, but couldn't wait.
We would have sat in the living room, her favorite
blues and greens, she would have feasted her dying
eyes on you, her daughter's intended. Afterward
you and I would have gone for a walk, feeling
our escape into the chilled fall air, my guilt
walking with us.

Now that she's gone I feel her near at times,
and today I feel that she is grieving over
the news of our divorce. I thought you might
like to know.

# Proud Flesh

I am the scar of my parents, not their child,
except so far as tearing flesh apart
makes one both mother and daughter to the wound.
It's so late now to make this feeble start:

But all I ask is health enough to go on,
not balm of Gilead, true healing — could
this world offer such stuff? From night till noon
I stagger as I may, as any would

who found herself around after the fray
of childhood ended, still hurt, always alone.
By speaking now I hope to find a way
to soften angry edges, or atone,

so healed or not, the proud flesh and its ache
hold life beyond that long ago mistake.

# Troy Jollimore

Troy Jollimore is the author of three books of poems: *Tom Thomson in Purgatory* (2006), *At Lake Scugog* (2011), and *Syllabus of Errors* (2015). *Tom Thomson in Purgatory* won the National Book Critics Circle Award. As a philosopher he has authored *On Loyalty* and *Love's Vision*. He has published poems in the *New Yorker*, *McSweeney's*, *Poetry*, *The Believer*, and elsewhere, and has been the recipient of fellowships from the Stanford Humanities Center, the Bread Loaf Writers' Conference, and the Guggenheim Foundation.

# The Arrow Man

Nate was in the natural foods store, reading the label on a jar of allegedly organic pasta sauce, when he felt someone's eyes on him. Turning to his right, he saw a very thin twenty-something woman with a gray T-shirt and unwashed hair, looking at him like she was trying to place him. He had seen this look before. He knew what was coming. He went back to the pasta sauce; there wasn't any point, really, in either making an issue of it or trying to avoid it. When she moved away he felt relieved, assuming she had given up trying to figure out where it was she'd seen him before. They sometimes did. But a couple minutes later, in the dairy aisle, there she was again, and as she moved past him, though he refused to meet her eyes, he felt the frigid heat of her glare.

She leaned toward him, whispered into his ear. It could have been a highly pleasurable and intimate gesture. In different circumstances.

"Asshole," she whispered.

"I'm not him," he replied, weary of the whole damn thing, though he doubted that she heard him, or understood.

He finished his shopping, paid up, left. He had only been in the store twenty minutes or so, but in that time the clear sky with which the day had begun had been overtaken by storm clouds. Medium-sized drops of rain were arhythmically spattering the sidewalk. He had every right to go to the store, to buy his spaghetti sauce and lemon yogurt just like everybody else. Her hostility was irrational, he knew that. But hostility clings to you when it's felt so strongly, as if you have walked through a spider web. He paused on the corner to take out his cell phone and dial his parents' number — the number, that is, of the place were they were, or were supposed to be — knowing there would be no answer. Sure enough, there was no answer.

He walked around the neighborhood for fifteen minutes or so — he was not yet ready to go home, that place had its own set of perils — before the rain grew intense enough to drive him into a Starbucks.

"Short cappuccino, please."

The barista scrutinized his face. "Hey, aren't you — ?"

"No."

He took a table in the corner and sat facing away from the room, putting his bag of groceries by his feet. He used to try to explain it to people. But most people wouldn't stick around long enough to have anything explained to them, and if they did they were either incapable of taking it in or else were too embarrassed by the stupidity of their mistake to admit that they were in the wrong. In the old days, when the whole thing began, it did not happen as often as it did now; maybe two or three times a month, which was, admittedly, still frequent enough to be irritating. James Kirsch, back then, was known to television viewers for playing Azimuth Azure, a sexy, elegant, thoroughly amoral doctor who, in his clinic after hours, conducted nasty blood transfusion experiments on unwilling patients. The sort of experiment no reputable Human Subjects Board would even consider approving, at least not in the real world Nate shared with seven-plus-billion co-occupants. The show was The Undead Chronicles, a one-hour drama broadcast weekly on the Showtime network, and Azimuth Azure was a vampire; and both the show and the character had, idiotically, become very popular indeed. Moreover, and sadly for Nate, it turned out that a surprisingly large number of the American TV watchers who were idiotic enough to enjoy the show, and helped make it so idiotically successful, were idiotic in another way as well: they were as bad at discerning the distinction between Nate Findley and James Kirsch as they were at discerning the distinction between fiction and reality. Not a majority of American TV viewers, to be sure. But not a negligible number either. Well above the threshold for statistical significance. Enough to carry an election, say, if the circumstances were right and the system a little bit fucked. Which was surprising, given the level of delusion involved. No matter how a person might resemble an actor who plays a vampire on TV, it takes a special species of crazy to believe that the person standing in front of you in the Pasta & Sauces section is a vampire.

"I'm not him," Nate would say, gently, patiently. "In fact, nobody's him. He's a fictional character. And also, as it happens, I'm not even the actor who plays him. I just look like the guy. You understand? I'm twice re-moved. I'm not even an actor at all. And also, I shouldn't have to say this but I will, there's no such thing as vampires."

He used to say this. But he had found it to be pointless. The people who were confused enough to make this sort of mistake weren't go-ing to have their misaligned view of the world corrected in the space of a few sentences. These people, who apparently thought their TV sets, laptops, iPads and Samsung Galaxies were live feeds to somebody else's reality, were committed to their delusions. There was no setting them straight. He was beginning to think that they had no desire to be set straight. They seemed to enjoy thinking of the real world as something delivered via technology, something electronically mediated that comes through a screen, as opposed to matter, the hard, physical, resistant stuff that made up and surrounded their actual bodies, the stuff that held their bodies up and buffeted them around.

Of course there were also many people who did not think that Nate was a vampire, but simply that he was James Kirsch. Those people, back in the early days, were on the whole respectful; many kept their distance, others would approach and compliment his performance or ask for an autograph. This was mildly irritating but not, in the grand scheme of things, a big deal. But after The Undead Chronicles com-pleted its run, when things should have gotten better for Nate, they instead got much worse. Kirsch's next career move was, for Nate, disas-trous: he joined the cast of a reality TV show, I'm Not Acting, one of a dozen formerly successful but currently unemployed actors who were moved into an imitation Italian villa somewhere in the Hollywood hills so that whoever actually watched such shows could chronicle their long declines and hopeless attempts to reignite fading careers in entertaining detail. And as it turned out, the 'real' James Kirsch — the one the camera captured week in, week out — was an absolute jerk: pretentious, arrogant, and embarrassingly and at times revoltingly ignorant regarding even the simplest, most basic matters of politics, culture, or science — all of which, for some unknown reason, he considered himself an authority on and insisted on pontificating about on every possible occasion. Suddenly the people who in coming randomly across Nate in some public space or other believed that they had just made a James Kirsch sighting were no longer so respectful. They stood and whispered excitedly, rolled their eyes and made mocking gestures with their hands, or sent texts to their friends like Guess who is standing in front of me in the line to see Anomalisa? That asshole James Kirsch. And their friends would text back things like, Anomalisa? Someone will have to explain it to him afterward LOL. Or, Make sure to ask him why he thinks that schools were better when they were segregated. Yes, James Kirsch, in addition to his various other charming personality traits, was a racist. He was the "I'm not a racist, but…" kind of racist, one of those "You know, some of my best friends are black…" racists. One of those — yes, he was on record as having said this — "Really, though, it's not as if everything the Klan stands for is bad" kinds of racists.

It was all so very unfair. Why couldn't he resemble a celebrity people liked? Why couldn't he have turned out to be an indistinguishable replica of Ryan Gosling? It might at least have helped him get laid from time to time. Of course Ryan Gosling was good-looking; a person who looked like Ryan Gosling would be able to get laid, presumably, even in a world in which Ryan Gosling was not a celebrity. But then again, James Kirsch was good-looking, too. All actors are good-looking; you don't get cast to play a vampire if you aren't extremely attractive on the outside, no matter how blackened and corrupt your bloodthirsty character's heart might be. So, since Kirsch was good-looking and Nate looked like Kirsch, it stood to reason that Nate must be good-looking too. There was a name for that inference, that he had learned in college:

the Identity of Indiscernibles, Modus Ponens, or the Law of Transitivity. Something like that. Why, then, was it so hard for him to get laid?

The cashier at the natural foods store had been wearing earbuds, grooving on her own private musical world. Was she allowed to do that? It seemed to him a gesture of contempt toward her customers and he couldn't help but take it personally, as silly as that was. It had nothing to do with him, after all. She just wanted everyone to know that she wasn't really there, that she would soon be somewhere else, that in her imagination, her heart, her true self, she already was living somewhere else. As if she were performing her job remotely, like one of those pilots who sit in an office building in Virginia and drop bombs on people in Afghanistan, then stop at In-N-Out on the way home for their daily Double-Double, animal style. A drone cashier. Or else it didn't mean anything at all, it was a just a thoughtless act, expressing nothing. Nate knew he was far too young, at twenty-seven, to start feeling like one of those old men who see the young as thoughtless, brainless hordes whose behavior expressed nothing and who sought nothing but the shallow consumerist pleasures of the moment. Indeed he did not want to become one of those elderly cynics, now or at any age. But he could see that it was happening to him anyway, that it had already begun to happen and that the conclusion was inevitable.  He used to resent older people for the weary and angry dismissiveness with which they regarded the young, their odious nostalgia for the bright-eyed and intelligent and squeaky-clean young people who, in their idealized memories, populated the America of ages past. Now he could see his future self, a small, stooped, withered man — a man who looked very much like his father, truth be told — raising a clutched cane over his head and squeaking Damn you whippersnappers. No damn respect. Why I oughtta.

And who could blame him for taking the side of the aged, when the young were as they were? Case in point: just this morning, in the museum of contemporary art, a young woman, about twenty-two or so, had asked him how you found out the prices of the paintings. She didn't understand the concept of a museum, apparently. Or perhaps it was simply the very idea that something in the world might not be for sale that refused to accommodate itself to her capitalist sensibilities. Jesus, was he a Marxist? He had never read Marx. Was it necessary to read Marx to be a Marxist? Or maybe a Marxist was something one might become inadvertently, without really intending to. Like becoming an alcoholic. Was that how it worked?

---

Why *was* it so hard for him to get laid? When he was single, nothing ever seemed to happen for him: trying to interest women in going to bed with him was like trying to set fire to bales of damp hay by staring at them and imagining, as vividly as possible, a cigarette lighter. As for relationships, they nearly always followed the same pattern, starting out good — the sex was decent and reasonably frequent for the first month or so — then entering soon afterward into a period during which the line representing the frequency of sexual bouts (he always pictured it as blue, his favorite color) slid at first gently and then precipitously southward, while the multiple red lines that stood for various symptoms of relationship trauma — heated arguments and shouting matches about stupid, typically trivial matters; evenings of reciprocal frustration and incomprehension whose conversation-less silence was laced by a resentful, barely suppressed hostility, leading inevitably to endless uncomfortable nights during which each of them would migrate as near to their edge of the mattress and thus as far from the consoling warmth of the other's body as possible; days when one or the other partner would disappear for some hours and, when they finally allowed themselves to be located, would respond to inquiries about where they had been and what they had been doing and with whom with a half-hurt, half-angry "What's it to you?" or "Since when do you care, anyway?" — rose toward the top of the page like slowly inflating bread dough or, let's not pretend the comparison can be avoided, a slowly engorging penis, and then, having achieved a certain critical momentum, shot madly skyward like a helium balloon released by a careless and now tragically disappointed child who had just the moment before sincerely, even passionately averred that he could be trusted to keep a firm hold on the string, that the one thing he would never do was let it slip from his fingers, which of course is precisely what he had just done. Before too long, inevitably, he would find himself mired in a draught as inexorable and as soul-depleting as the one that had been afflicting the state of California for several years now. Women, he had concluded after some years of fairly trying experience, did not really want sex. Nor, he had come to believe, did most men. There was a great deal of talk about sex, which might have led one to believe that people were in fact having it, or at least interested in having it — the culture, if its media, art, and everyday talk were to be taken at face value, was obsessed with it, in one way or another — but, rather than being a concomitant to the activity, all this talk had instead somehow come to replace it. As one of the few people left on Earth who actually enjoyed fucking, he seemed to belong to an unpopular and presumably dwindling minority. He ought to find others of his kind; they should hold meetings, organize mutual support sessions. There should be government-sponsored programs to promote their interests and ensure their fair treatment, to assist in their assimilation into and proper functioning within a mainstream society that was in so many ways openly opposed, and at times downright hostile, to the values for which they stood; to preserve a selection of their number, perhaps, so that, in the far future when conditions were more amenable to their existence, they could be re-introduced, as part of a pilot program, into the wild.

He had had coffee with his current girlfriend, Tracy, earlier that day. Current and soon to be ex, or so he supposed. The coffee date had been, in part, an attempt to plug the holes and set aright the sinking ship, though by this point he was not entirely certain that he wanted the holes plugged: this particular ship might in fact be more comfortable, more at home, at the bottom of the sea than floating on the surface, exposed to the heavens and the gods that lived there; and that life raft, with just enough room for one and surely some delicious rations stuffed away somewhere onboard, was looking awfully appealing right about now. That said, there was no denying that Tracy was in many ways a very good romantic partner: bright, funny, and what's more a talented actor — indeed there had been increasingly frequent signs in the past few months that she might be on the way to becoming that rarest of things, a successful actor. Though of course that would only lead to trouble, in fact it was already becoming a source of trouble, since Nate, although he saw himself as a highly ambitious person and had tried his hand at many things — he was an aspiring playwright, an aspiring pianist, an aspiring composer, it's what he did, he aspired — had yet to be particularly successful at anything. He seemed forever stalled in the aspirational stage, when of course the very point of aspiration was that it aspired to something else, was that it was meant to lead to something non-aspirational.

Also, of course, it had been nearly two months since they had had sex.

They met in the café at the Guggenheim. She was coming from a meeting with an independent producer who regarded herself as an artistic rogue (she could not speak about herself, it seemed to Nate, without repeatedly using the phrase *avant-garde*; moreover the woman wore an eyepatch, and not, he was fairly certain, for legitimate ocular reasons) and who was potentially interested in a one-woman performance piece Tracy was working on; in an hour she was due in rehearsal for the Tom Stoppard play she would soon be appearing in, in which she played an actress who was having an affair with a playwright. (When Nate had said to her, "Ah, life imitating art," she had frowned and blinked, signaling incomprehension, as if it had slipped her mind that he did, in fact, write plays. Then again, maybe it had slipped her mind that the two of them were romantically involved.) She had, as usual, "made time" for Nate, wedged him in between theater-related events. She was wearing a skin-tight black leotard under a very short black skirt; he had to admit that she looked remarkably sexy. If she had been a stranger he had spotted at random in one of the galleries he would have thought God, I'd love to fuck her. Fat chance of that. Which of course was precisely the thought that entered his mind when, with a cup of coffee and a slice of carrot cake in front of him — he had gotten there early, he had wanted time to sit quietly and prepare, to consider his strategy — he looked up and saw her entering the café. The fact of her being his girlfriend notwithstanding.

Still, he *had* fucked her. She had wrapped those beautifully sculpted legs around him and closed her eyes and sighed. He had even made her come, a number of times. He wished, now, that he had kept track, that he knew the exact number. But it was something. Even if he didn't know the number, even if the number wasn't going to get any larger. With her, and maybe, who could say, with anyone.

"Hey Nate." She sat down.

"Bonjour, mon petit camarade. You look fetching. Do you want something?"

"I'm good. They had snacks at the thing."

"So how did it go?"

She told him it had gone well, that the producer seemed genuinely interested. He wasn't surprised; the piece was good. He'd read it, the current version, and she had performed bits of it for him. The fact is, he admired her talent; he'd been with women before with whom he'd had to fake it, the admiration bit, but she was the real thing, or at least stood a good chance of being the real thing. Aside from her beauty, her overall sexiness, that was the thing that stung most about the idea of them breaking up. Although actually it was more complex than that: her talent, her being the real thing, was part of her sexiness, part of her beauty. It was what made her worth having, and it was a huge part of what was driving them apart.

"You'll never guess who I saw on the way over here," she said.

"Who?"

"You don't want to try to guess?"

"I hate guessing," he said. "Just tell me. Who?"

"James Kirsch."

"You've got to be fucking kidding me. Please tell me that you're fucking kidding me."

"I almost walked up and hugged him from behind. Or yelled out, hey sexy! I'm lucky I didn't grab his dick or something before realizing it wasn't you."

When was the last time you thought about grabbing my dick? he couldn't stop himself from thinking. But he did stop himself from saying it, at least. He was still, at least for now, someone who could exert that much self-control.

"And then when it realized it was him I wanted to tell him what a wanker he is. And tell him that he was ruining my friend's life and he needed to fuck off."

The use of the word *friend*, rather than *boyfriend*, did not escape Nate. It did not strike him as a good omen.

"He really does look a lot like you, though. I know you don't like hearing that, but it's true."

"I know it's true. I'm the first to admit it. We're goddamn twins."

"Well, maybe on the outside. You're completely different from him as a person, though. Thank God. So what have you been up to today?"

"I've been here, pretty much. I've been looking at the art." Indeed, he had spent the previous two hours standing in front of paintings. It had taken him a long time to learn to look at paintings; now, when he could get himself into the right headspace, he found it a deeply profound and relaxing experience, but when he couldn't he felt their immobility, their refusal to enter into the constant flow of time and change, as an affront. It was so different from the type of art with which he felt most comfortable, which existed in time and moved: a play, a film, a dance, a piece of music. The kinds of art that, explicitly or implicitly, suggested a narrative, the kind that used rhetorical devices to carry their audiences through a sequence of movements, of competing and developing ideas, each idea given its own voice, its own signature or character or instrument, starting quietly and then building to something complex and frenetic, then perhaps resolving into something peaceful and reassuring, but all the while acknowledging their mortality as things that took place in time and did not strive for an immortality that was both impossible to achieve and, let's admit it, unworthily immature to strive after or long for. This was, he often thought, the main thing that he still enjoyed about city life: the contrasts, the rich, evanescent, constantly mutating patterns formed by the panoply of distinct and competing voices, sometimes consciously interacting, sometimes singing their individual and idiosyncratic songs with no attempt to harmonize with one another and thereby creating rhythms and harmonies that could not have been planned or intended by any singular composer, no matter how skilled. To begin the day in the placid island of his Upper East Side apartment — well, his parents' Upper East Side apartment, but he preferred not to split hairs — then plunge into the nervous and unconstrained energy of the city streets and the subway, and from there to the silent stasis of the museum; it was the kind of structure he appreciated, the kind of progression he would strive for when he himself would attempt to compose music or write a play.

Now he had fallen into the habit of spending a great deal of his time among paintings and sculptures, artworks that did not move at all, that did not acknowledge the passage of time, that remained utterly and obstinately silent and still. "The silence of the truly talented musician," Mr. Mariana, his piano teacher, used to say to him, "is not like the silence of an amateur. The artist plays differently than others, of course; but when he does not play, that too is different." It was the sort of wisdom some people climbed mountains to hear. Or so it had struck him at the time. Now, when he stood in front of a painting and heard his teacher's words in his head, he found himself wondering if he had been taken in, if Mr. Mariani had not really been a huckster at heart, simply passing himself off as a sage. Who was he, really? Some friend of his father's, though he did not figure that out until somewhat later, after two or three years of lessons, when he happened to walk in on the two of them enjoying a drink in his father's study, laughing merrily like a couple of old industrialists who had found some clever way to evade some government regulations or to force their employees to spend most of their paychecks buying their own worksuits from the company store. "Yes?" his father had said to him as if his presence in his own home was surprising or somehow inappropriate. "What do you want?" What they actually had been laughing about he had no idea, but he felt somehow that it concerned him. As if the entire attempt to teach him to play the piano — yet another thing he aspired to — was a plot of some sort, a weird ruse. At any rate, all those insightful observations and pearl-shaped dollops of wisdom had not, in the end, been of much use. He never managed to compose a piece worth playing or listening to, nor did he learn to play the piano with the grace and emotion of a master. He was barely competent. His silence still sucked. Unlike Tracy, whose career was clearly going somewhere — her whole being seemed to consist in the act of going, in the fact of her not ever being static or still — Nate, it seemed, was going nowhere.

Tracy was talking about her piece, she had been for some time, while his inner focus had been drifting from one thought to another. The particular problem seemed to be finding the proper space for the performance. "I should be surrounded by the audience," she said. "So that there is no way out for me without going through them. No escape. They should feel that they have that kind of power over me. Ideally it would be on a floating stage, in fact we'd all be floating, no stable ground beneath us, just water. Maybe I could be isolated on my own little floating island-stage. I could swim out there, to the little island, to start the performance. That would be kind of ideal, artistically, but also pretty impractical. And cold."

"It's all about compromises, I suppose."

She looked at her phone. "I really don't have much time. I'm sorry I was a little late. Was there … something you wanted to talk about?"

Everything he had planned to say to her had dissolved. Faced with Tracy's beauty, her inexorable, almost assaultive desirability, he wanted to say only Be with me. Stay with me. Except that he also wanted to say Stop hurting me and Leave me alone, and these requests would not have gone well together. So he just sat and said nothing.

She said nothing, too, and several seconds ticked silently by. At last she moved, as if to break the uncomfortable spell, and said, "Really, I do need to go."

"Tracy," he said, "are you okay?"

She paused. "Why in the world would you think I'm not okay?"

He considered the question. He had actually meant to ask, Are we okay? but had not been able to make his mouth form that question. Perhaps it felt too vulnerable, like a request for reassurance. Or perhaps it made him too complicit in its implication that whatever it was that he, and surely she, was sensing was not okay was not entirely centered on her but included him as well.

"I am okay," she said. "I am very, very okay. Things are really great with me. I feel good about my work, other people are starting to feel good about it too, I can actually see the outlines of the career that I've been wanting — "

"I know," he said. "I know you're doing great. I'm really happy for you."

"Then why do you do things like ask if I'm okay? Why do you look at me all the time with this look of … this look of concern? Like you're thinking, what's wrong with her? Why is she acting like that? What's going on? Because I tell you what's going on. I always do. When something's going on, I tell you."

"I know that. But I feel this distance between us."

"That's coming from you. The distance is coming from you. In fact, the distance is inside you. You've got something inside you, you drive everyone away. You drive yourself away from yourself, even."

It had gone downhill from there, proceeding in short order to a list of Nate's faults and shortcomings, of which, in her eyes, there were many; chief among them, of course, being that he was a twenty-seven year old man still living with his parents, that he had never achieved terms of peaceful relations with his father, that his first question to himself, when faced with any significant life decision, was What would Mother want me to do? (It was not the first time an accusation of that nature had found its way to her mouth. She had been known, time to time, when she was truly pissed off and wanted him to hurt, to refer to him as "Norman," meaning, they both knew, Norman Bates.) It was all entirely unfair, of course, certainly the bit about him "still" living with his parents; as he pointed out, "still" implied that he had been living there continuously, when in fact he had lived elsewhere for several years and was at any rate not now living with his parents nor even, really, living in his parents' apartment, but rather — and the distinction was crucial — house sitting for people who, yes, happened to be his biological progenitors, while they enjoyed the European tour they had looked forward to for some years. It was a business arrangement, one that benefited them as much as it did him; if anything he would prefer to be living somewhere else, he was doing them a favor. But this defense, as cogent as it was in his mind, only precipitated a further barrage from her, in which phrases like "false consciousness" and "Peter Pan" made unwelcome and memorably pain-inducing appearances.

As for the bit about his mother, he let that one go. It had stung, and it was unlikely he could have addressed it, in that moment, without realizing how much it had stung. They would discuss it later. If he could manage it, and if they were still together.

They did quite a good job, he thought later, of keeping their voices pitched to a reasonable level. The people sitting at nearby tables did not, as they ordinarily might have, abandon their seats and move to calmer, less emotionally fraught territories. A couple of them, who were more attuned than most to the language of look and gesture, or else were simply eavesdropping, were aware that a fight was taking place, and did that looking–like–I'm–not–at–all–interested–when–in–fact–I'm–quite–interested–and–wish–I–could–hear–just–a–little–bit–better thing that people do. He couldn't blame them. He would have been interested too, had it been some other couple. Truth be told, he would have tried to listen in and then, at the first available opportunity, would have written down some of what he had overheard for use in one of his plays. He had always struggled with dialogue. At any rate, when, twenty minutes later, Tracy left — late for her rehearsal, which surely pissed her off greatly, and which he undoubtedly would hear about the next time he saw her, assuming that there was a next time — the two of them had, together, taken yet another step toward the breakup that now seemed quite a bit more, rather than less, inevitable. It was the precise opposite of what he had intended their little coffee date to accomplish. He would have been better off avoiding her completely. Maybe that, he thought to himself as he was passing through the museum exit, was the only way to make a relationship with a woman work. Just make sure that you never actually talk to her or see her.

———————

At the end of Season 3 the writers of The Undead Chronicles killed off Azimuth Azure, which should have been Nate's salvation — or so he thought at the time; and indeed, it's quite possible that if Azure had been allowed to remain dead, which is, after all, what decent people do when they are dead, Kirsch never would have found his way to I'm Not Acting and Nate's life would have been rather different. But the show's fans rallied and, after a well-organized and highly enthusiastic letter-writing campaign (why, Nate wondered, couldn't people turn such energy to saving the rainforest or putting up to date textbooks in elementary classrooms?) the character was quite literally resurrected. One of the advantages, it seemed, of working on a show about undead characters was that when it is necessary to bring one of them back to life, it is an easy thing to do. No particularly clever writing stratagems are required; one need not invoke a heretofore unknown identical twin or an elaborate CIA-sponsored conspiracy, let alone the "it was all just a crazy dream" gambit. All that is required is a little ritual: a broken cross, some wolfsbane, a vial of Unholy Water, and a few words muttered in the moonlight, or whatever other ridiculous formula a roomful of T.V. writers can concoct.

Nate found himself thinking, now, as both his latte and the rain outside dwindled, about that five-month period of hope, his initial elation at hearing that Azure had been killed (he had never been able to bring himself to watch the show, but friends began calling as soon as the vampire's body hit the floor, pierced by a stake and spilling blood of unknown provenance on the Persian rug onto which the stricken body had fallen), the despair that followed when he realized that they would be bringing the character back. And then he thought about Tracy, pacing around his house — this was just a few nights ago — in costume as Annie, repeating over and over, but with varying intonations and emphases, a single line from the Stoppard play: "I didn't know you were on the train."

"I have to go out," he had said. "I can't listen to those words one more time. You're making me sick of those words."

"I didn't know you were on the train," she had responded, twisting it in a different direction this time, giving it an interesting combination of irritation and tenderness, an amalgam his interpretive faculties could not quite penetrate.

The rain was letting up. He decided to go. He didn't suppose she would be coming around tonight, but if he turned on all the lights in the place, and the television, and put some music on the stereo, it might not seem unbearably lonely. His parents would complain about the electric bill when they got back from their trip, but it would not bankrupt them, and what was money for if not to make the world seem a bit cozier, a bit more hospitable to human life?

The weather had fooled him; halfway home it started raining again, quite heavily. He put his hands on top of his head, as if somehow that would keep him dry, and ran as quickly as he could. As he turned the corner onto his parents' block he realized that his hands were empty and should not have been. He had left the grocery bag, with the pasta and sauce, a dozen eggs, and a few other necessities under the table at Starbucks.

"Fuck," he said. "Fuck fuck fuck fuck fuck." He repeated it several more times, tried giving it different intonations, the way Tracy had with her line. It made him feel mildly better, but no act of uttering fuck, regardless of the quality of the delivery, was going to bring his groceries back. It seemed embarrassing, somehow, to call and ask one of the baristas if anyone had turned in some organic pasta sauce to their Lost and Found. And what about the eggs? Could he ask them to refrigerate them until tomorrow? Would they be safe to eat if he didn't? Or he could grab a coat, a hat and an umbrella from home, walk back to the coffee shop and retrieve the bag. Or eat whatever he found in the cupboards at home — surely there would be something, though he couldn't remember, really — and call the groceries a lost cause. That would involve a loss, but at least it would show that he was the sort of person who could let go of things, who did not hold on tightly out of insecurity and fear. As he went over these various options in his mind he was walking up to his parents' building, and it was at about this point that he noticed that the lights in their ground-floor apartment, which he had been intending to turn on, were already on, and that there was music coming from within.

He went inside. It was just remotely possible that his parents had come home early, though if so, why hadn't they warned him? And when he passed through the hall and looked around the corner into the dining room, he saw a dozen or so people who were not his parents sitting around the long wooden table. He recognized no one. One of them, a man at the head of the table, was holding a tumbler in the air, he seemed to be in the midst of giving a toast, and when he noticed Nate he stopped and simply looked at him, directing at him a somewhat inscrutable expression. It was perhaps, Nate thought, a slightly surprised look, mildly puzzled, but not as surprised or puzzled as it ought to have been. Nor, for that matter, was it nearly as surprised or puzzled as Nate found himself feeling at that moment.

"Well hello," the man said. "I see, can I help you?"

"I'm not sure," Nate stammered. "I believe — perhaps I have the wrong house."

But from where he stood he could see various small items — photographs, wall hangings, the calendar with his mother's comments and annotations in the red ink she preferred — that told him that this was, in fact, his parents' apartment, the place where they had lived for over thirty years. The place where he had grown up.

"Wrong in what sense?" the man asked.

He tried again. "I believe — " but he had no idea how to finish the sentence.

A woman in her thirties, in a black and white dress, who was sitting beside the man at the head of the table, smiled at him. "Why don't you join us?" she asked.

"I don't think — "

"Oh, please," she said. "The least we can do is show you some hospitality."

Surely it was he who ought to be showing them hospitality? Or already was? Or was that what he ought to be refusing to do? But rather than attempting to challenge them, and their right to be hospitable, on this basis, he decided to try a different tack.

"Might I use the telephone?" he asked. He had taken great care not to say "your telephone," but had refrained from the challenge, not to mention the irony, that would have been implicit in "my telephone."

"Of course," she said. "Right this way." She stood and turned to the man next to her. "You continue, dear. I'll just take care of this and then I'll be right back."

She led him to his father's study, where there was, indeed, a phone, the last land-line in the apartment, perhaps the last one in the city. "Are you friends of … Wesley and Jill's?" he asked her.

"Wesley and Jill?" She thought for a moment. "No, I don't believe I know them."

"Oh. That's odd. That's … it's quite peculiar. You see, they own this apartment."

Now she looked genuinely puzzled. "Do they." She indicated the phone. "Well, I see. Please, make your call — and then, if you'd like to join us for dessert — "

"Yes, well," he said, "I'm just going to give them a quick call, if that's okay."

"Of course," she said, somewhat cautiously, as if he were someone she did not want to antagonize. "We'll be in the dining room. Please … give them our best." She left. He let himself sink into the leather club chair next to the little table on which the telephone was perched, and for a few minutes he just sat, trying to think of just what one says to one's parents in such a situation. While he was doing so a young woman in a black cocktail dress entered the room.

"Hi there," she said. "I don't think I know you. Are you with, ah, with them?" She cocked her head toward the dining room, where the rest of them remained. It was a very attractive head, Nate thought, well-formed, somewhat classical and nicely traditional — no visible piercings, tattoos, or other voluntarily adopted deformities — and framed by a corona of reddish hair that he judged it would not be unpleasant to run one's fingers through. Then he realized he had seen her earlier in the day. She had been standing in front of a de Chirico at the museum. The Red Tower. She had stood there for some time, silent and still.

"No, not with them. I'm not really with anyone. Also, I don't really know who they are."

"Mmm," she said, and sat down in a chair facing him. "I feel that way myself, sometimes."

"No, I mean — I'm not trying to be metaphorical here. Anyway look, I really need to make a phone call."

"Oh. So you'd like me to leave." She crossed her legs, causing the skirt to fall away a bit and reveal a pleasing degree of thigh, while simultaneously leaning back away from him. It was, he reflected, precisely the sort of move for which the black cocktail dress had been created. "But now, do you really want me to leave?"

He said nothing.

"Knowing what we truly want is so difficult," the Red Tower Woman said. "Perhaps you'd just like to relax a little. I could help you relax."

"I don't know what you mean. Are you offering — ?"

"I just mean, you seem a bit agitated."

"I have," he explained to her, "left my eggs at the coffee shop." When she did not seem to understand, he continued, "at Starbucks."

"Well, that does sound a bit unpleasant, I suppose. Can you get by without them? It appears that dinner is already taken care of. I could bring you some if you like. My name is Samantha, by the way."

"I don't know those people. I literally don't know who they are or what they are doing here. In my house."

"You don't really want me to leave, do you? Why don't I sit right here and wait while you make your call?"

"That would be fine," he said, a bit primly. He watched her rooting around in a handbag she had produced from somewhere as he dialed his parents' number. The phone ring a few times; then, surprisingly, someone picked up, and he heard his father's voice.

"Hello?"

"Dad? It's Nate."

"Nate? What's happening? Is everything okay? We're just up. What time is it there?"

"Dad, did you … did you give someone permission to have a party at our place?"

"I don't remember you asking."

"No, I don't mean me. I mean there are all these people here, having a dinner party. I don't recognize them. I thought maybe they were friends of yours and somehow … you forgot to tell me?"

"Are you sure you're in the right house?"

"Yes, I am. Look, I'm touching grandpa's inkwell with my right hand even as we speak."

"Touching it? Why? Is that helping?"

"I'm just …" The woman with red hair, Samantha, was beginning to look a bit bored. She craned her neck, apparently trying to read the titles of the books that lined the shelves of his father's study.

"They're probably friends of your mother's. I'm sure she knows what's going on."

"Can you check with her?"

"You know, Nate, now that you bring it up, I've been meaning to talk to you about our arrangement. Your staying in the apartment. I think maybe it's time — "

"Okay, sure, but Dad, could you check with Mom about this? This is a lot of people."

"Sure. She should be back any minute. She left about two hours ago to go down to the village and look in the stores for, I don't know, trinkets."

"Two hours? I thought you said you just got up?"

"I just got up. Your mother's been getting a very early start these days. To be honest, she's been acting a bit strangely. I told her the stores wouldn't be open this early. But you know, in any marriage that lasts this long you have to expect a certain amount of stormy weather."

Samantha got up from the chair and walked over to one of the bookcases. He watched her remove a small leatherbound volume, give it a brief appraising glance, and put it into her handbag.

"Ah, that's my father's — " he said as she left the room.

"What's that?" his father asked.

"No, look, I think I have to go. Could you ask Mom when she comes in? Or just have her call me here at the house?"

"Of course. Just remember, every relationship has its difficulties that you need to ride out. Just like with you and Tracy. Love isn't two people staring into each other's eyes. It's two people standing side by side, looking off into the distance. Together."

"That's beautiful, Dad."

"Like, at a mountain or a sunset or something."

"Yeah, I get it. And a genius's silence is different from a regular person's silence, right? I know." He hung up and went back to the dining room. A few people still sat at the table, but many of the others had left to wander about the apartment–; they stood about here or in nearby rooms, chatting, sipping at drinks. There seemed to be even more people than before. The music was louder, and he thought he could hear distinct, clashing music from upstairs. Through a doorway he saw the main couple, the ones who had been at the head of the table. The ringleaders, as he had come to think of them. They were standing by the fireplace. It took him a couple of minutes to make his way through the crowded room, but eventually he got there.

"Ah, hello again," the man said to him. "Were you able to make your phone call?"

"I say," the woman said, "you do look familiar. Doesn't he look familiar, Gordon?"

"I'm not," he said. "I look familiar because I look like James Kirsch. From television, that awful show. Those awful shows. But I'm someone completely different. You wouldn't know me."

"And you got everything worked out?" Gordon asked. "With your parents? Did you manage to retrieve your eggs?"

"No, I – the eggs have nothing to do with it. The eggs are a separate issue."

"Well let's not run everything together," the woman said.

"The eggs are indeed a separate issue," said Gordon.

"That they are," Nate said. "That they are. Look, I'm feeling a little bit lost in this  conversation. Have you — have you been talking to Samantha?"

The woman looked at him and narrowed her eyes a bit. "Samantha," she said to him, "is very skilled."

"Ah. That's good to hear. I'm pleased. In what way?"

"She is very skilled," she repeated. "You should take her offer very seriously."

"Do you mean skilled as a pickpocket? I think she took one of my father's books. Do you happen to know where she is?"

"You keep bringing up your father. But he isn't here, is he?"

"No, I just spoke with him. Does it matter? Do you have permission — ?"

"I say," the woman said again, "You really do look familiar."

"I look like an actor. He's very well known. He played a vampire. People think I'm him. Or they think I'm the vampire. They don't understand the difference." He looked down at the tips of his shoes. "To be honest, it's driving me crazy."

"That's simply how things are," Gordon said. "This is where we are. As a country. Do you know about the Arrow Man? He was a fictional character who appeared in advertisements for Arrow shirts. A fictional character. Based on a number of different models. They were paintings, I believe. Not photographs. The point is, the Arrow Man, although he did not exist, received thousands of letters from fans. Proposals of marriage. And of less savory things."

"This is where we are," the woman said to him. "This is the country we live in. People would prefer an illusion over reality. They just want a show."

"So people think you're a vampire," Gordon said. "People will think what they think. Own it. Use it."

"But I'm not a vampire."

"You're not a vampire, and you're not James Kirsch. So what are you?"

"I don't know." He thought. "I might be a Marxist."

The phone was ringing.

"Do you think it's possible that I'm a Marxist?"

"Well, what are your feelings toward capitalism?" the woman asked.

"Fairly negative."

"Then I'd say it's possible."

Nate excused himself, went to the phone and picked it up, hoping, though he knew it would not be, that it was Tracy. It was his mother.

"I talked to your father," she said.

"Great. So can you explain what's going on here? All these people?"

"I was not buying trinkets. I know he said I went to the village to buy trinkets, but that is quite inaccurate."

"Mom, I don't care. I just want to know, are these people friends of yours?" He was standing by the front window, looking down at the street. Samantha was standing on the front steps.

"What people? What's all that noise? Are you having a party?"

"Mom." He thought hard. He wasn't sure what to say. "Have you heard of the Arrow Man?"

"The Arrow Man? What did your father tell you?"

"No, this has nothing to do with — "

"Marriages are complicated. That's all I'm saying. I mean, have you ever known me to have an interest in trinkets? Really?"

"I really don't — "

"Anyway, we really need to talk about this 'house-sitting' arrangement of yours — "

He put down the phone and went outside. Samantha stood to the left of the steps, leaning on the railing, smoking a cigarette. He took the same spot on the other side. She smiled at him.

"I didn't know you were on the train," he said.

"Nice party," she said.

"Mmm. Well, it's a nice place."

"Is it yours?"

"Ah, well, I suppose I'm wondering that myself. But you know what they say. It depends on what your definition of 'is' is."

"That's an enigmatic comment. Do you always talk in riddles?"

"You ask a lot of questions. I think it's my turn to ask a question, isn't it?"

"Very well. One question. That's what you get. One question, to which I will truthfully respond. You can ask anything. You could ask me about my philosophical or religious beliefs, or who I vote for. Or you could ask, what have I got in my handbag? Or, don't I know that smoking is bad for me?" She took a drag, held it for what appeared to be a long, pleasant moment, then exhaled a long plume of smoke, which the same breeze that had been playing with the little tufts of her hair that curled around her ears now gently pushed into a pleasingly interesting crescent shape. A parabola. He recalled the word from math class, ages ago. "Or you could ask, am I seeing anyone? Or any of a thousand other things. So many possibilities. But you only get one," she said, "so choose carefully."

He leaned against the railing, staring at the cracked pavement of the street, at the corner of the yard where a little free-spirited local breeze was play-ing with a discarded plastic bag. He had spent much of his childhood on this street, playing silly games with the neighborhood kids, exploring that weird, volatile mix of aggression and affection that adolescent boys con-struct friendships from. He had had his first kiss here, just a few feet from here, on the sidewalk, with a girl whose name he no longer remembered. In fact all he remembered about her was that she had long straight brown hair, that she smelled like kitchen spices, that she rode a boy's black bike — he had liked the bike and even coveted it a little, it had possessed, some-how, the mildly threatening aura of a stealth bomber — and that her father owned the neighborhood hardware store. She had kissed him, and then run away, and nothing had come of it. But she remembered that smell, a mix of cinnamon, vanilla, and something a little bit peppery.

"Have you got one?" the Red Tower Woman said.

He looked at her — direct, a bit challenging — and she did not look away.

"I'm thinking," he said.

Photo by Suzanne Engelberg

# Lorna Stevens

Lorna Stevens is a mixed media artist who lives and works in San Francisco. She makes books to tell stories and alters found objects to make new visual comments. Her work has been acquired by the Brooklyn Museum, di Rosa, the New York Public Library, the Numakunai Sculpture Garden, and the SF MOMA Research Library. She received her MFA from Columbia University and teaches collage and sculpture at City College of San Francisco.

For this issue of *Nostos*, Stevens created two diptychs. The first, *Growth Chart, Younger and Older,* derives from photographs of the wall where she chronicled the heights of her children, family and friends. (Photographs by Mika Sperling) The second diptych, *Cross Purposes,* comments on the challenges of parenting.

Ben 12/2/98

Emma 9/29/02

Emma        BEN 4/26/98   5/29/02

BEN    9/16/97    Emma 11/10/01

Emma        4/3/96

Emma  4/17/33

EMMA  2/17/00

EMMA  8/3/99

EMMA 11/5/98

Rich 12/2?/16

Cole 12/26/16

Ryan 8/15/?

Ryan ——— 8/19/05
Ben 6/23/05

Alexa 12/26/16

Emma E 4/3/06

Katie 6/9/05

Meg 6/29/05

Kelsey 7/14/05    Meg 12/31/04    Ally    Katy 4/?/06
                  7/18/05

Emma 12/24/05

Ben 5/?/0?

Colley 12/13/04

Ben 4/26/18    5/29/02

Emma

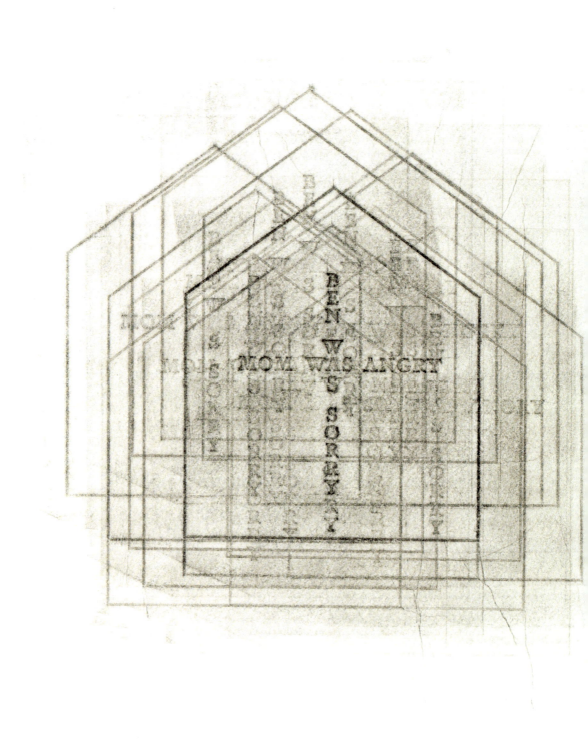

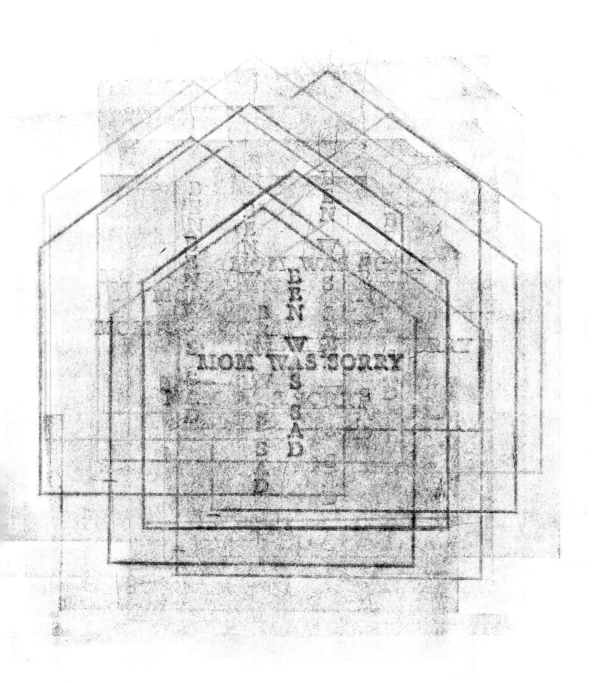

# Keleigh Friedrich

Keleigh Friedrich lives and plays in Northern California, splitting her time unevenly between the Sacramento Valley and the Eastern Sierra. In Sacramento, she handles crisis communications for a national animal welfare non-profit, practices yoga and astrology, and lives with her partner and their Guatemalan rescue dog, Maizey. In the Sierras, she hunts for hot springs and imagines the planet before humans intervened. Keleigh received an MFA in writing from Mills College in 2009, where her thesis won the Amanda Davis MFA Scholarship Award. For the last 12 years she has served as a volunteer for the Awareness Institute.

# Wings Instead

My father thinks that human beings are not meant to be weak. He is the 1974 Petaluma Wrist-Wrestling Champion, an aerospace engineer, a soccer coach for young girls and adult lesbians, someone who believes in materials science and propulsion. He claims that people are not meant to be plush as bread loaves, transparent as ciphers. We are made of muscle and matter, he says. We are dense and powerful as bulls. But some of us behave more like crustaceans.

Dad says that we have strayed from our birthright, which is to be rulers of this kingdom, claiming our dominion over animals of less divine origin.

"There was a holy transaction that occurred in the Garden of Eden," he says as he tears up dry roots and the rotting flesh of wood planks in the yard of my dead grandmother's house. He says it was not merely the fall of humans to a postlapsarian state of sin and sorrow, it was a symbolic shift from one species' reign to another. Before the rise of mammals, reptiles ruled. Dinosaurs, yes, but also reptilian birds, fierce serpents, enormous amphibians. The earth was a playground of soulless creatures: slimy, writhing, merciless. What do you see when you look into a reptile's eyes? He answers himself: Nothing remotely human. You see a black well, going straight down to nothingness. Why else was Satan embodied in the form of a snake? There's a reason for everything, he says, for every little thing, if we can just go beyond our puny ten percent brain power. All dots can be connected, no matter how distant in spatial understanding. When our foremother bit into the fruit of the Tree of Knowledge, she was entering a contract, rife with immitigable responsibility; an agreement to take over as stewards and ambassadors of the planet. What ensued was a passing of the torch from reptile to mammal as Alpha Beings over all other things living and growing.

"Most crawling reptiles have stayed the same for millions of years," he continues. He is sweating profusely through his white T-shirt, making half-moon stains beneath his armpits. "They're the most earthbound of all creatures, condemned to eat dirt for eternity. But some evolved into gravity-defying aeronauts, they grew feathers and wings and transformed into birds, symbols of freedom. They said to hell with crawling or walking and transcended that step entirely."

"Why didn't I?" I want to know.

"Why didn't you what?"

"Why didn't I skip crawling or walking and grow wings instead?"

"Ah," he says, squaring his hands on his hips and squinting into the cypress-treed distance. He tells me that upside-down I spilled onto dry land, a rapid evolution from amphibian to mammal. I went from the impersonal caterpillar silence of the umbilical cord to the protruding softness of my mother's nipple. That, he says, is a cosmic miracle if ever there was one.

I don't believe him. He hasn't been sleeping much the past few months since Grandma died and Mom left – he is obviously a little crazy. What could be more miraculous than flying? If I could hold my breath like the jellyfish, like the ones in the Hudson River that I once peered at through the slats of a wooden pier, well that wouldn't be so bad. I could go backwards, devolve to my pre-mammalian state. "Those are lion's mane jellyfish," my father had told me then. We were on a six-week business trip on the East Coast, parlayed into a family vacation, and I had the maddening habit of floating off to make them look for me. The jellyfish were a mystical distraction, gooey apparitions trailing rust-colored entrails just beneath the water's surface. I lay out flat on the sun-warmed pier, one cheek pressed hard against the wood, myopic gaze hypnotized by their soundless ballet.

"Then I should have stayed upside-down," I say decidedly. It all makes sense — the countless hours I've spent practicing cartwheels and handstands on the sidelines of Erin's soccer games, the time in kindergarten I attempted to hang by my ankles from the uneven bars, my proclivity for hanging off the couch with my dirty feet against the pillows to flip the television screen on its head.

"Maybe you are," Dad says. He heaves a stack of fallen tree branches into the refuse pile behind him. "Maybe we all are. Maybe this whole world is upside-down and the ground is really the sky and the sky is really the ground. Did you ever think of that?"

I did not.

"You just never know," he says. "Anything is possible in this crazy world, anything at all."

I sit bow-spined and squinting in the harsh light of the afternoon. This day is the longest I have ever experienced. We are cleaning out my grandmother's house in Tarzana, a dusty ranch-style house on a shrubberied street that ends at the right-of-way of the Southern Pacific Railroad. Murph, Erin's boyfriend, is helping my father tear down an old shed. My sisters are collecting the empty animal cages and putting them all in a corner of the yard — next to the stone pool that my father says used to hold piranhas — to be taken to the dump at day's end. I am perched on the edge of a dirty marble birdbath, watching, convinced I am eternally exempt from anything so common as labor.

While my father and Murph and Erin and Minnie (those two the more robust of my three sisters, the ones who stand in for sons on the soccer field and in the garage) tear up rotten shingles and dismantle cages and remove woodpiles, I drift through the house, inspecting each dim and antiquated room. Grandma's house is wild and overgrown, a study in benign neglect. It's a zoologist's home long after the animals have done their mortal time, their bodies buried beneath the magnolia tree or placed in shoebox caskets and long forgotten on a closet shelf. A wooden swing hangs from a walnut tree in the front yard, made of smooth gray willow branches woven together like a basket. Inside, the house is always a bit too dim in daylight, always smelling of the emulsion of past and present, as peacefully out of time as a diorama. The rooms and grounds are populated by the animal spirits of their stuffed stand-ins, like the ones we see at the Natural History Museum staring motionless back at us through laminated eyeballs.

My grandmother was a packrat of the Depression-era variety, saving slivers of bar soap and outdated magazines. She still had her rotary wall telephone, her bulky Royal typewriter, her rusty mailbox painted garishly like a toucan. In her tiny bedroom I finger piles of gaudy jewelry — clip-on costume earrings glowing sapphire, rhinoceros pins and owl brooches, bead necklaces whose colors emanate the heat of African plains. I remember Grandma sitting in the driver's seat of my father's Astro van, that certain way she applied lipstick in the rearview mirror, the lipstick saffron-red the color of Arizona dirt, rubbing her fleshy lips together, closing and opening them with a culminating smack and rolling the lipstick back into its silver tube.

The bed in Grandma's room is made, the comforter olive-green and folded primly with the covers tucked beneath the plump of pillows like a matron's dress caught beneath her bosom. I can't picture Grandma sleeping here, all alone after Grandpa Jim's death, with the night trains shaking the windows at midnight and the nocturnal cries of the animals dwindling year by year as her menagerie shrank, died off, and finally ceased to exist, leaving only Sheba the blind mutt running into furniture in constant pursuit of his mistress.

The only other bedroom is my mother's, but it looks nothing like my mother. Here is where she slept in a cushioned bureau drawer until they could afford a crib, and then in the rigid twin bed covered in washed-out pink flowers. But there is no sign of the mother I knew, or even the myth of the mother I knew. There is no black and white photograph of Beverly smiling in her drill team uniform or walking down the aisle on the arm of the short, russet-haired teenager who can't contain his Luckiest-Man-Alive grin. He wore me down, Beverly said later. He helped Daddy with the animals and eventually I just said yes and then again yes and then the final all right, I do, yes.

On the night before their wedding she slept here with her best friend Caroline and nearly forgot to feed the animals. Her parents were away in Europe, always away. While Beverly was making her rounds a skunk got her, sprayed her with his stink. She stayed up half the night bathing in tomato juice, again and again to eradicate the smell, and told herself there is no such thing as omens.

In the tiny den I find a mechanical pencil and a memo pad half-filled with grocery lists. I flip past *Campbell's cream of chicken soup, brown sugar, black shoe polish, three-barb fishhooks, Crest toothpaste*, written in a loopy cursive resembling my mother's. I imagine the black shoe polish was not for shoes at all, but for painting a furry black bat blacker, and the fish-hooks were to string the bat onto a fishing line, to play him painlessly for a movie camera. I see my grandfather taking a sleepy little troglodyte from its cage and stretching its wings to span the length of my arm. "I'm gonna be working this bat for a vampire-dog movie," I hear him say. A forelock of silver hair, still thick and shiny, flops over his right eyebrow. His eyes squeeze nearly shut when he smiles, one side of his lips droop-ing slightly to reveal a slug-pink tongue too big for his lopsided mouth.

The den is stacked on all sides with books and *National Geographic* magazines and photo albums of their travels. I sit at my grandmother's cluttered desk, before her ancient pea-green typewriter, which I do not know how to use. I feel at home amidst old things. They smell of a past wherein the *I* as I knew it did not exist. I can hear my father out-side calling orders to Murph and my sisters, his philosophical orations temporarily ceased. Tonight when we get home I will sleep with the blind Sheba in my arms, even though she's flea ridden and whimpers in her sleep and will soon be put down, unceremoniously, after which my father will come home with his eyes red-rimmed and rheumy. I want to reread Genesis and see if there is any hint of God going back on his word that humans are fated to dominate. Perhaps Jesus told us later some variation of *"Just because you can…doesn't mean you should."*

The empty refrigerator hums at my back, a backdrop of color curtains my mind – a vespertine golden blue like the November sun through the eucalyptus trees at dusk — and then words come with a rush of ecstasy, the quiet euphoria of a homecoming. They are words about tumbling out upside-down, landing on fins and sprouting legs, trading gills for lungs. They are memories of breathing underwater, drifting the surrendered seas like jellyfish in ballerina skirts, mothers who untether and float away, never to be seen again. The words are grey and then violet, tawny-yellow and seafoam green, and finally the ferrous red of blood and sand in an unsuspecting mouth. The words smell like skunk and feel like empty cages, and by the time I've written them all down I feel as eternal as a fly in amber, ready for the Santa Ana winds to carry me home.

# David Rollison

David Rollison moved to San Francisco in the late summer of 1963 to study with Kay Boyle, John Gardner, Leonard Wolf, Jack Gilbert, and others. After teaching poetry, first in Santa Maria, California, and then Marin County, he retired, living on the edge of San Pablo Bay where it intersects the Petaluma River. He and his wife walk the bayland wetlands every morning, in the morning mist, along with the egrets, the coyotes, the Canada geese, the quail, the turkeys, and the red wings. Sometimes, in the afternoon, he can write a poem. His recent collection is *Ghost Poems & Wetland Ballads*, and he has published several poems in early editions of *Nostos*.

# My Mother's Ghost

A girl in a worn photo on a foggy pier
with her hair bobbed, holding one hand
with her other hand, her skirt fanned
in the breeze that ripples the ocean or lake
surrounding her.  A lone figure
sits at the end of the pier. He may have nothing to do
with my mother. Or it might be my father
sitting small and far away. It looks like his back is to her,
so he's watching the water or fishing maybe.
My mother's a young woman with all the fires of life
in her face and body. Her message
as the girl on the pier can't be deciphered.
All of that is dead now.

# Watching Dance with the Dancers

I always knew there was dancing.
My parents danced the ballroom dances:
My handsome father with his black,
slick hair and his pencil thin black moustache,
my pretty mother with her Andrews Sisters hair
and shapely calves—they
could dress up beautifully and go out dancing to "Peg o' my
Heart,"
their cocktails on a white tablecloth
at their table near the bandstand.
Somehow, I got to be there. Maybe
they told me about it or maybe they took me along sometimes.
I think I remember the white tablecloth
and the cold celery, the radishes,
the kidney beans spiced with horseradish,
the Roy Rogers cocktail, but I can't be sure.
Always at the front of my mind, though
is the smoky bandstand, the gleaming coronets,
the saxophones, the clarinet, the snare drums,
the crooner's bent kneed posture. Then
there is nothing but the song which says,
"*We looked at each other in the same way then,*
*But I can't remember where*
*Or when.*" And my parents dancing.

# James Tipton

James Tipton is the author of *Annette Vallon, A Novel of the French Revolution* (HarperCollins, 2008), based on the true story of William Wordsworth's great love. It was a *San Francisco Chronicle* Bestseller and a Barnes & Noble Discover Pick. Tipton has also published poetry and short fiction; recently, "The Vampire of Edinburgh" and "Shiva's Eye" in *Alfred Hitchcock Mystery Magazine* and "The Lieutenant at Dachau" (based on his father's experience at the Dachau War Crimes Trials) in the literary magazine *Blue Unicorn*. Gary Snyder called Tipton's book of poetry, *Sacred Places*, "keen, taut, and skillful."

# Jettisoned

The way you described
how the pioneers going west
would lighten their load
letting go of a beloved old
dresser or a cast iron stove
or pan that had cooked
a thousand meals they might
need them again but now they
had to make it through the pass
you told me this after your first
stroke sitting there together by
the wide flat slow river that
reminded you of the Platte
you said you had seen the
wheel ruts you had crossed
that mile wide inch deep river
and seen also some things left
behind under the grass now
an old pan one drawer of
a dresser you said this in your
slow way after your stroke
and now you are free of all
things jettisoned as unnecessary

cargo and you come weightless into
my dreams last night I even
introduced you to the Pope
I said Pope this is my father
a World War II vet I thought
that would impress him

# Where She is Now

Between two redwoods
where there's a view of the bay
       and Tamalpais

for the living
a bird calls
       sun on my face

I close my eyes
       and feel the veiled rays.
       now only wisps of cloud

in a sunset glazed on the bay
       as we drive west towards Tamalpais and
       only the fleeting glint of gold

between sky and mountain
       know her being
       fresh now in the twilight winter breeze

# Grace Marie Grafton

Grace Marie Grafton's most recent book, *Jester*, was published by Hip Pocket Press. Six collections of her poetry have been published. Her poems won first prize in the Soul Making contest (PEN women, San Francisco), in *Bellingham Review*, and The National Women's Book Association, Honorable Mention from *Anderbo* and *Sycamore Review*, and have twice been nominated for a Pushcart Prize. Ms. Grafton taught with CA Poets in the Schools, earning twelve CA Arts Council grants for her teaching programs. Recent poems appear in *basalt, Sin Fronteras, Pirene's Fountain, Canary, CA Quarterly, Ambush, Peacock Journal*, and *Mezzo Cammin*.

# Learning and love

They are in the land of the dead,
these fictional characters and I
must leave them there until
after my father's funeral.
The book will bring its heroes back
to the living.

My granddaughter chooses
a birthday party over her great-grandfather's
death.  A brighter-colored dress
and, recently, white for her aunt's wedding.

The ants got to the guinea pig's
corpse before her teacher found it.
"The worms and bugs will eat him."
She wants birthday candles
and too-sweet frosting.

We will bring candy to the funeral lunch,
dump it into a cut-glass bowl,
foil-covered fingers of toffee,
chocolate creams (the dark and
the light) wrapped in scotch plaid.
My brother will put out cherries
from his orchard.  He drove Dad
between the rows last May
and our father reached out the truck window
to touch the still-green, pendulous fruit.

# Meryl Natchez

Meryl Natchez' most recent book is a bilingual volume of translations from the Russian: *Poems From the Stray Dog Café: Akhmatova, Mandelstam and Gumilev*. She is co-translator of *Tadeusz Borowski: Selected Poems*. Her book of poems, *Jade Suit*, appeared in 2001. Her work has appeared in *The American Journal of Poetry, Poetry Northwest, The Pinch Literary Review, Atlanta Review, Lyric, The Moth, Comstock Review,* and many others. She is on the board of Marin Poetry Center.

# Theodicy

### or *How Evil Enters the World*

Sleep-deprived, confused, your nipples so sore
you can hardly bear the baby's ruthless gums,

and if she cries, you pick her up again,
and wander the few rooms your life has narrowed to,

the soft floss of their hair, the bluish pattern that blooms
under transparent skin, the tiny nails so fragile

they bend when you try to cut them. Soon
they begin to know who you are, they reach their chubby arms

towards you, they smile, they nuzzle the soft bones
of their fontanel into your neck,

and there has never been anything more delightful,
not sex, not the best meal, not driving fast

in a convertible on a winding road by an azure sea,
and you would do anything for them, and you do,

you give up nightlife, adult conversation, hour-and-a-half
massages, spicy food, uninterrupted thought,

and they learn how to walk,
to swim, to read, and you've paid for the orthodontist

and endured the teenage years, and paid for college and
helped out with grad school and they're launched,

with their own lives, their own ways of salting meat
and slicing it, their own partners and opinions,

here they are, flawed human beings with adult problems
for which it turns out you are the cause.

# Sharon Pretti

Sharon Pretti lives in San Francisco. She works as a medical social worker at Laguna Honda Hospital where she also runs a poetry group for seniors and disabled adults. For many years Sharon taught poetry workshops at assisted living facilities in Marin and San Francisco. Her work has appeared in *Spillway, Calyx, MARGIE, The Bellevue Literary Review, The Comstock Review, The Healing Muse* and other journals. She is also a frequent contributor to haiku journals including *Modern Haiku* and *Frogpond*.

# Chemotherapy and the Park

The man beside me on the bench
says it's called a flight,

the lifespan of a monarch, the miles traveled
to reach the mountains of Mexico.

The butterflies don't have maps in their brains
explaining which route they should take.

I don't tell him my brother wants to make it
all the way to 60. Three days on, ten days off.

I don't say he'll try anything,
his doctors using *contain* instead of *cure*.

Monarchs cluster together to stay warm,
I'm told, tens of thousands, more wing than tree.

This is the spot I return to each week,
witness how everything is in motion—

milkweed, thermals, the wait for favorable winds.
There's still so much we don't know

is how the man says good-bye,
the cap on his head unable to keep his hair from flying.

# On the Lake

Because I ask, my mother shows me the trail
she and my father used to take

before they knew they'd be parents,
before the years worked fault lines between them.

She's sure this is the spot where they used to stand,
hands around the railing of the bridge,

his dark waves combed back,
scooped neck showing off her collarbones.

Less overgrowth back then, she says,
and the glitter light leaves on the lake

didn't make her sad.
She hasn't let *lymph node, metastatic,*

*my son* land in the same sentence yet.
Still vivid: scraped knees, long division,

the lunches packed in paper sacks.
She says there's an order and she should be first,

her voice clear, a stem snapped off.
The path is narrower than she remembers—

blackberry vines, monkey flower,
what can and can't be touched.

# Karen Poppy

Karen Poppy has work published or forthcoming in *The American Journal of Poetry, The Gay and Lesbian Review Worldwide, ArLiJo, Wallace Stevens Journal,* and *Blue Unicorn*. She has recently compiled her first poetry collection, written her first novel, is at work on her second novel, and is an attorney licensed in California and Texas. She lives in the San Francisco Bay Area.

# Graveyards

Hush for a moment,
And listen.

We know enough
About each other
To fill a graveyard,
That's how well
We've dived in.

Sometimes my anger
Expands like an ember,
Rips up the earth.
At those times,
I fear worse
Than a graveyard.

Apocalyptic fire.
Wind-spit fury.
Graveyards
Giving up their dead.

After all,
I don't even know
If you're sorry.

# We Hold Each Other and Remain Here

Even in the blistering of our names,
Hot-rubbed by their contempt
And chaffing whispers, we hold what's ours:
Each other. The coolness of your throat,
A river's song against which I bed down,
Soothed by its rise and fall, susurrations.

If our names are wounds, let them break open.
Still, they try to drown us in them,
As they drowned your father last summer.
Our names, our wounds, our dead
Define us — but still you calm me
In all this aching heat. My family,
Already gone, cold in a cold forest clearing.
Your family, most of them escaped.

Why do we remain here, defiant?
Our names a pus-curse on this town, and
All who inhabit it. Our arms pretend
That strength and love are all we need
To survive. The house still stands.
Someday, you will want nothing of it.

# On Your Birthday

*for Cecily, who was like a sister to me*

I never knew the name of my earthly love
Until you were gone.

Because that love is friendship, a meal,
I savor the memory of your freckled limbs
And taste the age you will never be.

I sit in the doorway,
Crouched among leaves.
But your eyes twinkle with the last season,
And I sigh,
"Forgive me,"
Since you are gone but I continue.

Rain dampens the leaves, lacquers their mottled beauty.
I touch them as if they were slick skin
And swallow in their swollen scent.

Their veins open to the air,
Spread through their star-shaped bodies,
Glistening fire on my hands.

Such temporal brilliance.

Come winter, leaves under snow,
My teeth cold, and the air strongly mineral,
I will say your name
Against the pure, colorless sky.

# Joanne Esser

Joanne Esser writes poetry and nonfiction in Minneapolis, Minnesota. She has also been a teacher of young children for over thirty years. She earned an MFA in Creative Writing from Hamline University and published a chapbook of poems, *I Have Always Wanted Lightening*, with Finishing Line Press in 2012. Her work appears in many literary journals, including *Common Ground Review*, *The Sow's Ear Poetry Review*, *Welter*, *Gyroscope Review*, *Temenos*, and *Water-Stone Review*.

# Portrait with Lies

My father settles into smoke
at the end of each workday.
In his plaid, stiff-backed chair
he tells us tales of tall buildings
far beyond our window's reach,
peaks lost in a rainbowed sky.
My father drinks butterscotch rum
in a tall glass with ice
imported from bright islands where
no one like him would ever go.

My father sings with an open mouth
all the hymns his mother taught,
says Latin words he memorized,
*Gloria Patri, et Filio…*
when he was once an altar boy.
He bows down before the clock,
prays to keys and the television,
buries dollar bills in garden soil.
He flies to heaven on a plow
conjured from his boyhood farm.

He built our house of gray cement
without ornament or hinge,
sturdy when tornadoes blow.
My father goes to bed early,

though he says he never tires,
folds his hands upon his chest,
stares at stars straight through the roof.
When his dreams start tapping hard
on his forehead with demands,
he shoos them off like pesky flies.

# Pictures on the Wall

Though you'd never guess it, my mother loved art.
She'd take me to Chicago, just us two,
as if we were girlfriends, to see again
the French Impressionists, the Chagall windows,
all those luminous blues
and the orange that shadows them.
For a day or two, we'd breathe together
that cool museum air, hone a secret vocabulary
not shared by my father or my brothers,
synchronize our gaze, linger near our favorites.
Then good pizza, window-shopping, an expensive
hotel room, guilty luxuries we stole together.
The drive home always went by faster
than on the way there, our reluctant reentry
into artless days, disapproval weighing
like barometric pressure on our skin.
The only art on our walls was a farm scene,
a cliché in oils, pastoral and unchallenging,
painted by my father's priest-friend,
with its country road converging to nothing
in one-point perspective.

# Heather Altfeld

Heather Altfeld is a poet and essayist. Her first book of poetry, *The Disappearing Theatre,* won the Poets at Work Prize, selected by Stephen Dunn. She is the recipient of the 2017 Robert H. Winner Award with the Poetry Society of America and the 2015 Pablo Neruda Prize for Poetry. Her poems and essays appear in *The Georgia Review, Lit Hub, Narrative Magazine, Conjunctions, Pleiades, Poetry Northwest, ZYZZYVA, The Los Angeles Review,* and other literary journals. "Disneyland Dad" is her first short story to be published since 1997.

# Disneyland Dad

Divorce — the ease of it, the simplicity of cancelling a relationship, as though it were really not much more than a financial transaction, a sandwich served on rye rather than wheat or a defective electrical appliance under warranty, had left Sam feeling faulty, as though he had been purchased, returned, and radically discounted, reshelved with a bright red sticker: *Price Reduced!* He had unknowingly been planned for obsolescence, and by the time he realized he was being tossed in the bin to be reappropriated as a boyfriend to some yoga-practicing grad student or as a single father destined to die early and alone, it had been far too late for a meaningful protest. Marriage, like all things of the consumer era, was disposable, and by default, their children felt the sense of being ignobly discarded, schlepped from one parent to another as though they were packages in the mail. At nine, Denise's ear had been particularly well-tuned to the discordant voices during the last year they had all lived together in the house he himself had built, and she had suffered from watching his gradual evisceration by jealousy and rage and the loss of his manly status in the household. Now he was doomed to an indefinite period of abject loneliness, especially detectable to those under ten. "Don't cry, Daddy," she said, more than once, producing a painting, a homemade card, a stem with one wilted poppy, a handful of grapes. "*I'm still here.*"

There had been a year of explosions, accusations, suspicions. Of reading Kate's receipts, of looking through her pockets, her purse, the underside of her car seat, actions that might be referred to by an outsider as stalking — such a cheap and vile notion, *stalking*, as though he were following her to her car (he hadn't) or popping out behind a produce display while she gazed at the ingredients on a bottle of shampoo (another level far below him). He had — and he would freely admit this on the stand, coolly, and with composure — taken her hard drive once, early on, paying one of his smarter, savvier day laborers to download files onto a jump drive so that he could just get at the truth of things. He wanted to know — or thought he wanted to know — what it was about him that was so repugnant. But after a careful examination of her writings, his main conclusion was that there was absolutely no way to unsee the words she had written. If she had only characterized him as evil or vile! If she had only exaggerated beyond a doubt her claims, then he would not have had to stay awake at night wondering where exactly the truth did in fact lie! What remained after reading were glimpses, images, and no way to un-know that his first nemesis — a certain Dale Carpenter III, son of *the* Dale Carpenter--had a back that his wife had poetically described in a letter as "an endless savannah of pleasure."

And so his life had tilted, taking a direction he'd not foreseen in any visible world. He moved into an old artist warehouse called The Quarry by its residents, although none of them mined or unearthed anything for a living save their pallid talents. Nights at The Quarry consisted largely of banal drunken conversations about nihilism and the fascist dictates of modern architecture, neither of which Sam had an opinion on; he was, however, happy for the company, and merrily toasted to this or that avant-garde heigh-ho as the opportunity arose. The Quarry was one of the only buildings standing next to a five-foot deep, 30-foot radius circular hole that separated the street from the river. The locals rumored that the hole was an alien landing site back in the 1970's. "Look how not one thing'll grow there," they still said, marveling at the gap in the earth, which filled with swampy water in winter and served as a mosquito breeding ground come spring. Denise and Duncan came every other weekend to "visit," as the custodial agreement stipulated, as though he were a Big Brother rather than their own father. The studio apartment — if you could call it that--overlooked both the alien land-ing site and the river. It was furnished with a hot plate and what the landlord had advertised as a "quarter bath" but was just a toilet and a sink, no bathtub or shower. The children had to bathe in a stock tank in the basement which the residents referred to as a "mikvah" due to its use by a Rabbi's wife three decades ago. Two holes had rusted in its sides, which Sam stuffed with tube socks to prevent leakage in the rab-binic ship. He had tried, both from an erotic standpoint and a spiritual one, to imagine the nude wife of a rabbi, bending over to wash herself, easing into the water which had to be delivered from an equally rusted nearby sink, five-gallon paint bucket by five-gallon paint bucket, until it was filled to a depth sufficient for the communion with God. Down between the pipes and the coils, amidst the blue light of the hot water heater, even her ghost seemed lovely, and he liked sitting with his imagined presence of her in a religious silence, watching Duncan and Denise flitter in the tank like wet sparrows, splashing as quietly as two children could splash in the grim darkness beneath the rooms where his neighbors painted murals or smoked weed off their balconies.

Sam hoped, at the very least, that the life he was now inadvertently providing for them at The Quarry was legitimately counter-cultural, that this strange spot he had come to inhabit might at least ensure that neither of his children would bear even a faint resemblance to their conventional mother. The aura of Sartre and cigarette smoke would surely render them more honest and thoughtful and intelligent, intrigued at the future prospect of living on the fringe rather than in the haughty suburbs Kate preferred. To this end, he fed them organic snacks. He learned to cook elementary pasta dishes. He took them to the laundromat, where a social life he had not known existed proved far more engaging than the sterile approach to laundry in the home; hookers snapping gum to dryers on high and the hygienic homeless who came to wash a load and sponge themselves in the restroom. He took the children to school on the back of his Vespa until Kate protested in the form of a restraining order and a request for full custody, at which time he bought them their own bicycles and they rode together as though he were a Papa in a French film. *There's a name for this*, Kate hissed at him when she saw them climbing off the Vespa after his first long weekend with them, watching as they ran toward the house with new pencils embossed with their names, each adorned by a bobbly elf, yelling, "Momma, look what Daddy got us!"

*It's Disneyland Dad Syndrome. You're turning into a real goddamn Disneyland Dad, you know*, Kate said, spitting the words at him, wiping a particle of her own spray from her impeccable outfit. Kate had taken to dressing as though every day were an outing to the Convention Center. She had lost weight, cut her hair so that she resembled a very sexy pixie, taken a job selling houses, which she was apparently quite suited for, all that falsity, all that pretention, all his own expertise in contracting benefitting her. "You'll notice here the coving around this doorway is a rich walnut," he overheard her say during a kid exchange, caressing the arch slightly as the buyers followed her, enchanted. He hoped that these contracts would eventually break, that each home she sold would enter escrow only to be found inhabited by a secret society of termites.

*They're pencils, for chrissakes, Kate*, he'd said. *Elf pencils. Don't you think that's a little bit of a leap? An exaggeration? You think I rode them to Disneyland to pick out a pencil? You think I'd ride them for forty-five minutes each way on a Vespa to go to a theme park full of spoiled children for fucking pencils? You think I can afford that now, with the support I am paying you?* He regretted this last remark, which indeed fell into the Divorce Cliché Collection, and he knew full well what she meant by "Disneyland Dad." A popular term amongst the several therapists they had seen together during the parting procedures and the subsequent mediation, a cautionary tale amongst the newly divorced. It was why he made Denise put her shoes on the shoe rack and why Duncan was supposed to round up the dirty laundry at night. He was not going to be so easily characterized. And he was not about to be out-theorized in the parenting department. He believed wholly that the situation they had been put into — the stock tank, the Vespa, the mornings in court — were a temporary setback, something that they would all wake up from years from now, when he and Kate were just getting ready to select joint burial plots, and there was little he was going to do to jeopardize that.

★

He'd met Kate in college. They ended up in a Vitaculture course together, which took care of his Ag requirement. What Ag had to do with mitering tile or using Excel remained as mysterious to him as the glow of Kate, who sat beside him every day, not looking in his direction, but glowing, nonetheless, her profile luminescent. They were lab partners, charting the Ph of wines, tasting them, learning the ins and outs of corks and foils. After two months of class and a not-insignificant amount of mutual seduction, they had ended up sneaking into the Vitaculture lab together one night, due to a defective latch he'd noticed on a window, proceeding to get drunk on what turned out to be a vinegary cab, past its prime, that had taken little to intoxicate them.

*I love wine*, she said, swirling the last of it in her glass, leaning in toward him. *And I think I am falling for you, Mr. Samuel Rogers.* They kissed deeply, in the same seats they sat in while class was in session. He proposed, after a heated, lengthy session of making out, that they find somewhere more comfortable. They walked out — stumbling, really — beneath the neon moon, arm in arm, kissing, kissing, and lay in the field where fellow students played rugby during the heat of the day, rolling on top of each other in a romantic swirl, a swirl that was to be repeated, over and over, hundreds if not thousands of times over the eleven years they would spend together. A piece of her hair ended up wound around his fingers that night, when he pulled at her curls in a fit of passion, and when he finally walked her to her car, eons later, the moon vacating the sky, he untwirled it and tucked it into the glovebox of his truck. It would, over the years, eventually dissolve until undistinguishable from the regular particles of dust that clung to handy men like himself.

Complications had arisen. In his way of thinking, however, they had been relatively minor. Perhaps, with the hindsight he had accrued over the last year or so, they had been of some consequence, but the daily annoyances of living together, raising children together, had been easy to ignore in the abstract. When Kate first came to him three years ago — he had just gotten home from work, not yet showered or changed, still dusted with the lint of Mr. Elder's dryer hatch — and said, "Sam, we've got to talk," he thought he knew what was coming. He thought he would end up taking on more dishes, or driving Denise to gymnastics without complaining; two of the more loathsome but necessary household tasks. But her opening remarks were, *This is not a marriage, Sam. You're not a partner, you're a child. Or an appendage.* Before he could respond — his heart and his throat and his brain combined into one little frozen, seizing muscle — she said, her voice quivering just a bit, *I want to be clear so you're not confused. I don't think I want to be married to you anymore.* The heart/throat/brain muscle burst into one horrible guttural sound. It was the same sound his boyhood dog Elmer made just before he died.

In the subsequent days — before he had found out about Dale Carpenter III — he tried everything he could to be less of an appendage. He tried arguing, countering, he tried one dozen red roses, he tried finishing the molding around the doors and the floors that he had long neglected and Kate had long nagged him to do, rendering the home he had built — largely, and literally, with his own two hands — now of commercial domestic quality. He tried calling his in-laws, who said colorlessly, "Eh? It's her decision." These attempts changed nothing. Then there was the terrible period of purgatory before he signed his lease at the Quarry, when he found himself sleeping on Gus' sofa, taking care of the children at night *in his own home* after he got done with work. Not only that, but Kate swirled around in tight sundresses in the living room — *their* living room — the one *he* had designed, for chrissakes — waiting for Mr. Dale Carpenter III, to arrive and sweep her up in his Grand Jeep Cherokee. In the end, with little reason, with absolutely no justice or recourse, he had become a refugee from his own home, his belongings dumped in the back of his truck as though he were a dusty Joad.

The truth of it was, once the relationship with Kate had gotten off the ground, Sam had never been very good at imagining the other ways his life might have turned out. Things had a way of happening to him without his specific consent. He floated along in the current of life enjoying the subtle sense of being carried, perhaps a result of having been the youngest child, pushed around in a doll stroller for the first two years of his life by his two older sisters. He'd aimed at being an architect in a vague and shapeless way, eventually demoting himself to design and finally, to construction management, largely due to lack of effort, drive, and multiple failures of nerve. He had been good at school, good enough that he was offered a chance on one occasion to accompany an archaeology professor on his summer travels to Romania — or was it Ruthenia? Somewhere in the eastern bloc — but he was missing some fundamental element, some sort of crucial motivation, and he never got around to beginning the process of obtaining a passport and visa. So he measured tiny closets when owners wanted walk-ins. He did room additions for families, adding on for the reluctant and sometimes unwanted child who stood in the doorway in terror watching Sam build the space where she would sleep alone instead of cozily inserted between her parents. He did kitchen remodels, replacing old linoleum with bamboo. He pushed windows out to look more closely at the seven square feet of yard that his clientele owned and cultivated, their own tiny facsimile of nature. But one of the deep, underlying belief he had about himself — which was now validated rather than contradicted — was that there was something wrong with him, something big, and internal, mechanistically wrong. From seventh grade on in his botched attempt to get Catalina McGuire to dance with him (she was right not to, he couldn't dance anyway) to canoeing (he never got the paddles quite right), to sex (how could he know, for certain, that he was pleasing someone *enough*?), he felt a great mantle of ineptitude upon him. He had clearly done marriage wrong; why else would Kate have deposited him so far from the life they had lived together? This particular wound seemed, if anything, to prove that his situation went well beyond some sort of faulty wiring. He was becoming more and more certain that the demise of the relationship was about 90% his fault. Marriage, and its companion, failure, were predatory in nature, and somehow, without his being involved explicitly in doing so, he had been prey.

★

Kate directed most of the details of the relationship, though, hadn't she? So would the failure be part hers? This was his focal rumination, an enigma that he felt, once solved, would lead to an eventual repair. It was like finding lost footings in the stripped foundation of an old house, or the remote fuse box hidden in the basement that controlled the light above the garage door — it would be an easy fix if he could only figure out the root cause. Marriage, children, the Ikea furniture he dutifully as-sembled in record time, and later, their divorce were all events that were orchestrated and conducted on her time line, at her prodding, and with her decorative flair. He had been better at living in her assumptions than his desires. She wanted them to marry (done), she wanted him to build them their own home (done), have two children (done), and learn to like, or at least tolerate, his father-in-law's peaty whiskey instead of Ken-tucky bourbon (in progress). When he dreamed — and he still dreamt of Kate, all the time — he repeatedly dreamt the same image over and over again. He liked to take it as evidence that clairvoyance might actually exist. The image was the two of them, thirty years in the future, lying in the shade of their woodsy back yard drinking iced teas. It made enduring this separation from her — extreme as it was — possible.

Once the children arrived — first Denise, then Duncan — he had brief, fleeting fantasies of a large family — children here, children there, all calling him "Papa." He sketched plans for adding onto the house dur-ing lunch breaks, parked in the cab of the truck; a room here, a room there, until the resulting structure looked something like the house of *The Waltons*. If he had any ambitions at all during the years he and Kate had appeared to be happy, it was of having a small farm run by a fleet of joyful children. The architectural structure of Sam's face even resembled that of the actor Ralph Waite, the sterling senior member of the Walton family. But really — and he would never admit this, even after the fire — having a family largely grew out of a lack of imagination for Future Sam, and it wasn't until the most recent turn of events that he had felt in charge of any particle of his destiny. Fathering was less art than mi-rage; it was a spectacle of pretending, of making believe that one could have an influence over the destiny of a small being in the world. Mar-riage, children, failure, flame. From here, now, he could see that his was really a little life.

★

He'd gotten to know a few of the residents of The Quarry during the rains, which had resulted in a significant drop in his employment. The alien landing site was pocked with small puddles and plastic bottles that bobbled during the storms. Late at night, when the children were with Kate — which was so much of the time, really — he would sit outside with the artists and the musicians, the writers and the wannabes, slapping at new bites with a drink in one hand, listening to their conversations, which drifted between indie musicians and politics and tattoo artists with waiting lists. He was lonely. Their lives seemed so full of direction. Even a tattoo involved a concerted effort at understanding and interpreting the self, a skill The Young seemed to have in droves. Ambition was on the same level of mystery as meteorology for him these days — were he to get a tattoo, what would it even be? He couldn't imagine. No totem called to him, no lines of poetry rang in his ears, he had no Celtic heritage, no love's name to engrave in a humoral field of roses. A hammer, maybe, although it would probably be mistaken for Communist propaganda. He often left these conversations early, wandering the long hallways that overlooked the river until he ended up back in his room to read. He had been going to the public library to check out a couple of novels a week, mostly Herman Wouk and Umberto Eco, bulky books he recognized from his father's nightstand. At Gus' prodding, he had checked out a copy of "What Color is Your Parachute?" and diagnosed himself as residing in the Realistic category in the six "Different Spokes for Different Folks" spheres, the most boring classification, indicating his aptitude and interest in Air Conditioning Repairs. Kate, he figured, was a combo of Artistic/Social, the two areas he most idolized in the colorful scheme of career reformation. It was no wonder she was a better person than he was. She possessed the necessary characteristics that made her capable of discerning the inertia he had for so long disguised as dormant ambition.

★

In the course of these balcony evenings he became intrigued by Melissa. She was young, probably in her twenties, making her equidistant in age from Denise as from him. She was a sculptor who carried a set of tools around at all times so that, if she were standing outside a café waiting for a friend, she might make a tiny figurine from the lump of saran-wrapped clay or chip at the brickwork in front of the pub to remind passersby of the unique power of artistic resistance. She wore loose overalls over a Sex Pistols tee shirt when he first met her; not sexy exactly, but so different from Kate that he was compelled upon first meeting her to ask, *What do you do,* and after she flirtily asked him the same and he told her in what he hoped was sweetly self-deprecating about the highs and lows of being a contractor. *Ahhh, so you make things with your hands. Me too. I'm a protest artist.* He liked the sound of that. It was a portal to something unfamiliar and purposeful, again representing the oppositional parachute slices of Artistic and Social. Plus her dedication to destruction sounded hot. He imagined hearing about the relationships between the squiggles she etched in clay and the crimes of the Bush administration after a session of energetic lovemaking. It turned him on. He lay awake that night, thinking of her short curls pressed against him, her shoulders shaking as she talked about Iraq and inkwells. He liked the idea of introducing her to Kate. *This is Melissa,* he'd say, his arm draped around her, lovingly, reveringly. *She's a protest artist.* His tone would imply, *what is it you ever did? How important, really, are you?*

The next time he and Melissa met, she came up to his apartment and knocked, looking to borrow a socket wrench. "Loose pipe?" he asked, and she said no, she needed it to bore eyes into a figurine. He wasn't wild about having his 5/8 crusted with clay, but he was wild about the idea of, finally, getting laid, and so he passed it to her, asking her to promise that she would show him the results. *I want to see,* he said, but as soon as the words hatched from his mouth he realized they sounded oddly lascivious.

"Sure," she said, rather tonelessly and without any real gesture of meaning. It hurt. He had not meant to be creepy, and felt a twinge of guilt at his lust, which had grown more out of a lack of sex than out of a specific interest in her — she looked too young, now, in the right light, her hair more stringy than necessary, her clothes so ragged they hung on her thin frame as though she were a dummy. He managed, nonetheless, to invite her in for a glass of wine when she came back upstairs, toting what looked much more like a cyclopsian turd than a figurine. She warmed to him a bit by the second round of wine. *I'm going to have an opening of my own in September. Have you ever thought of just, like, building your client a tiny house and saying, fuckit, I am not going to do one more palace for you fucking bourgeoisies pricks?* Still, when he took her empty wine glass from her — hoping she would lean in a little — she seemed more interested in making statements than on the pedestrian charms of sex.

After several more exchanges, Sam finally asked her to join him for a beer, out, away from the Quarry. He spent a lot of time nodding and listening to what amounted to an attack on the capitalist nature of art, sneaking to the bathroom at one point to Google "Marcel Duch-amp" on his phone. At the end of the pub date, he managed to kiss her, although she'd laughed afterward — a small laugh, but nonetheless dis-concerting, as though the joke was on him, and any moment a troupe of artists would come out, dressed in clown suits, mocking his feeble, conventional attempts at affection. *Relationships aren't really my thing,* she said finally, after he asked her — awkwardly, regrettably — how she felt about him. *They're about feelings, you know? And I'm less interested in my feelings than I am in, like, the larger feelings, the meta-feelings, the feelings about feelings. That's what art really is — trying to connect the feelings about feel-ings. I'm sorry,* she said, and it was sincere, or it sounded that way. Maybe, though, it sounded like she was relieved.

*Uh huh*, he'd said, feeling an overpowering sense of exhaustion drop down inside of him, a lump of dry ice that spread its smoke through each pore, each bone, each rivet of his musculature. It was an exhaustion not only borne of his forced period of celibacy, though surely it was that too; this was, so to speak, also meta, his body's recognition of how exhausting it was to spend months trying so hard to be hip and canny to the ways of the young. In his mind's eye he could see the protest piece she would construct of him, perhaps called "The Contractor," a mess of clay tools surrounded by jewelry wire with one cyclopsian 5/8" eye rutted in its center.

★

Gus was the only one of his friends who stuck around after the mar-ried friends had been divided and largely claimed by Kate, a few strays sufficiently frightened off by the year of sadness and expulsion. Gus was his primary carpenter. He was a master of the jigsaw, and did a lot of the cupboard work for Sam. He'd been to, as he called it, *Nam*, and a full third of his left ulna had been burned in combat, so that he worked slowly, a trait which had helped to solidify their friendship. Gus knew of the emails, he knew about the savannah of pleasure; Sam had crawled to Gus's first thing when she asked for a divorce, and lived in a fetal position for about three weeks before he could get it together to look for a place.

Gus could not stand the Quarry, though. *Goddamn useless hipsters.* He could not get behind the vibe, he said, of false despair. It was a bit of a rub between the two of them, so they had taken to meeting on Fridays at One for the Road to hash out the details of Sam's divorce and Gus's failed attempts at rehab.

*I have the weirdest dreams*, Sam said, three G and T's in. Gus had gotten up to drop two quarters in the jukebox, putting on Kenny Loggins, followed by Foreigner. The Quarry would never have permitted such musical choices. He told Gus about the dream of he and Kate growing old. *It's so real, it's so real. I don't know, man. Can't it mean something? Us growing old?  Like, why would that image keep coming up for me?*  Gus had little therapeutic expertise, but his answers were less canned and more thoughtful than those of the court-appointed Anger Management therapist he had seen during the last year.

*That's beautiful, man. But — I mean, I'm not a shrink, but someone might call it wishful---*

*I know.*

*Do you think there's any chance, Gus?  Like, any chance?  Like even a 1.3% chance that she'll come back?*  Sam asked, knocked back the rest of the gin, and regretted he didn't have it to sip on while he waited for an answer.

*I don't know, man. Do you even get any sense she's still into you?  Does she try to touch you when you go by to get the kids?  Write to you?  Does she give you any sense she's into you?*  Sometimes he would ask Kate, when he picked up the kids, "How're you doing?" in his most compassioned and sincerely conjurable tone, hoping for a bit of eye contact, a touch of her hand against his. She rarely answered in any meaningful way. *Fine. Did you include a check for the kids for lunches this month?* Once he had accidentally bumped into her in the hallway when he went back in for Denise's lucky pillow. He could feel her breasts grazing his back, and stood an extra second, hoping she might lean into him, let him rub his fingers against her bra as she used to like so well. Instead she said colorlessly, *I've got to go, Sam. Do you guys have everything you need?*

*Not really. I mean, who knows. I just don't understand where it all went. The relationship, that is.* Where did it fucking go? This question — put to Gus about 1,000 times in the last year — signaled the end of the conversation, because neither of them understood what happens when the life you knew simply disappears.

★

After Melissa there was Andrea. She played trumpet in a local jazz group. He'd never met a woman who played trumpet before, and when he saw her on the dish-shaped stage beneath the lights at the Concert in the Park, a community event that, since legalization, had become one giant dope screen with a few bagpipes or whatever instrument some fuck-up wanted to play, he was overcome with desire. While on stage, she looked out into the audience, one hand over her eyebrows like a sailor saluting the sunset, and caught his eye. She smiled. At the end of the performance, just as he was meandering up to see if he could talk with her a bit, a small boy beat him to her side, roping himself around her. His skin was much darker than hers, his hair flared upward in a tiny afro halo, and she lifted him up to toot one note on the trumpet. "Beautiful, Dizzy!" she said, and Sam's whole future flashed before him. Duncan and Dizzy in the stock tank taking bubble baths, a wedding in which the three kids gave them away. He imagined telling Kate of his plans to rewed. *I'm sorry*, he'd say, touching her shoulder lightly enough, and falsely enough, that he would be more therapist than ex, pressing his hand to her shoulder not as an object or subject of her love but simply as a messenger, a bearer of bad news. *All along, I never thought I'd find anyone, and here I actually did.* And he'd lean in to kiss Andrea, Dizzy standing above them, trumpeting an ode to their love.

After the concert, he hung around — he began to coil up some of the extension cords used by the sound team, to be useful — and when Dizzy, in a fit of exuberance, began to run off in the twilight, through the cloud of mosquitos, Sam kept his eye on the boy until he got close enough to the street to warrant concern, and then surreptitiously gathered behind him in dad-recon. "Hey there, not so close to the street, eh?" He sounded less like an agreeable version of a dad and more like a Canadian sub-uncle than intended.

*K*, said the kid.

*Where's your mom?*

*She's putting away her flute.*

*Can I walk you back there?*

Dizzy regarded him with something between disdain and familiarity, as though he were used to being followed to street corners after his mother's performances by men who ached for her. Dizzy's ease was such that Sam wondered if his presence at the gutter was purposeful, if he was sent out into the street, a man-magnet, to attract the one his mom had her eye on all evening long. Either way, Dizzy shrugged. *All right.*

Andrea's house was one of the many grandmother cottages that grew behind the glitzier homes of the college town. When she flicked the light switch, a ceiling fan began to mutter and swivel, its one bulb barely harnessed in its socket. "Go get ready for bed, you!" she said, nuzzling him and dumping him on the floor where her futon — surrounded by Guadalupe candles and a tiny postcard of Fats Domino — soaked up most of the room. Sam was both inordinately excited and already bored. This wasn't really a love-nest, but more like a glorified single-mother grad dorm, and it had the distinct feeling of being *well used*, as though a long series of men had urinated in the corners of this room, so that, even given Andrea's inescapable deliciousness — she had slipped into a silky dress and poured them each a gin and tonic — he was less turned on than he might have been. She was almost too comfortable with her sexiness, in love with her own carnality, the ease with which she operated men. But when she handed him his drink — her hand rubbing the back of his hand — the muted sense of excitement suddenly revved; the thought of that hand — and those lips, which had so beautifully puckered around the trumpet's brassy spout — made him inadvertently lick his lips. Embarrassed, he took a huge glug of the gin.

*Look at my poster, look at my poster!* sang Dizzy, from the other room, wholly undressed from the waist down, his tiny penis in motion as he jumped on his bed, a tiny pink hummingbird in flight, showing off a large poster of Snoop Dogg, one finger staring them all down. Sam felt like a foreign émigré, amidst the posters of another child, an impostor-father, missing out on this moment with his own children who were likely in the prissy, pristine bunk he had built-in for them at Kate's insistence, where she was no doubt reading *Stuart Little* to them.

*How's the single dad thing?*

*It's* — he could not say it, because nothing he said would not make him sound like a Christian, or weird, like someone who should know better — *rough. I miss my kids. I miss,* he wanted to say, *the rituals, the eggs benedict on Sundays, the orange tree in the yard giving off its predictable yearly oranges, the mail box, the real bath tub, the predictable holiday sex.* He had found himself crying the week before while reading an article about a Syrian refugee family, both at his own lack of perspective, and at the very serious and very real sense that while he was not fighting for his life or his political beliefs, he too was a refugee, expelled from his homeland, shipped to the shores of a UFO landing.

*I know,* she said. *Dizzy goes to Guinea to visit his dad every summer, and it is like my arm is missing, or my trumpet or something.*

*Ah*, he said.

*You were wondering why my little guy is black.*

*No, not really. I mean — yes — I mean?* What was the response he should choose? Should he go with *color-blind*? With the more contemporary *I don't see color?* It felt like there were a series of responses he should know how to offer, but didn't. She changed subjects almost immediately, asked him about his divorce. They talked a bit, the light intimate talk of those who are polite enough to pretend that the space between strangers is more than a direct line. He sipped the last of his drink, and she took it from his hand. *You're pretty fucking handsome*, she told him, kissing him on the neck, then the cheek, then the corner of his lips, a practiced routine. *And so goddamn strong. I'd let you build out my cottage anytime.* She led him to the bed, where he tried to shake the feeling of being a traveler who, late one rainy night, took refuge somewhere otherwise unconsidered, a train station, a pensione, and to let himself be comforted by the idea of what would come next. How it was that he had gone from suburban dad to back-house futon-fucker was a subject to be pondered during the ride back to the Quarry. For now, he managed to transform his shy erection into a sexy wand, which he used to make love to her with fortitude and a coppery desire.

★

It was his day with Duncan and Denise. He showed up five minutes late to pick them up, after nicking his neck with his razor in a hurry not to be late.

*Come on, kids*, Kate said. She stood at the door, holding it open, but not for his entrance, for their exit. She was dressed up. A shortish skirt. Her thighs, familiar enough, her scent familiar, making him think of how easy it would be to just — to just move her back into the house, pop a video on, and take her, crazily, like they used to, while the kids zoned out on old Scooby-Doo. Except that it would be easier to swim, naked, to China than to get her in bed again.

*Sam.*

*Yeah?*

*Um, there's something you might hear from the kids. God, I hate that they tell you everything.*

*I don't think they do*, he said, quizzically. He wished they did. The lawyers and mediators and therapists had insisted that he not pump them for information anymore, and he could sense, when he got too close to a particularly sensitive subject, that Denise in particular would become sullen, picking at her nails and chewing on them, a habit he disliked — his nails, being exposed to drywall, to insulation dust, were impeccably clean, and if he chewed at them — and who wouldn't like to? — he would end up poisoned after a month, no doubt, a victim of asbestos and TSP.

*Yeah?* He had his suspicions. One of the most painful things of late was that Dale Carpenter the Third seemed to have mysteriously vanished from Kate's life. And instead of calling Sam — and saying, *hey, would you like to try again? Would you, could we, try again?* she had begun dating a dad from Denise and Duncan's school. His name was Warren and he was plain and lumpy; he stood around with his hands in his pockets a lot of the time. He was an accountant for a few local restaurants, and the only visible draw to him was his wine collection, reaped as tips from the businesses whose books he meticulously kept.

*I'm — I'm —* she fidgeted more, and he liked that she was at least uncomfortable; it seemed to indicate, to him, a desire to preserve his feelings on some level. This was either very sensitive, or very pathetic news.

*Getting back together with the infamous Mr. Carpenter? I'm sorry, I mean Mr. Dale E. Carpenter the Third? Or maybe you've jumped the gun. You planning to marry Warren?* he asked, teasingly, or he hoped it sounded teasing, not like someone who had gone through her rubbish, looking for tossed-out bridal magazines.

*Pregnant*, she said. *Very unexpectedly so. And maybe. Marrying. Warren.*

*I see*, he said. Something weird was happening in his face; it was hot, and tingling. He felt like he might pass out.

*So the kids might mention it*, she continued, oblivious to the little seizure his heart was having. *Denise found my pregnancy test in the trash. I didn't want anyone to know yet until Warren and I* — she paused, almost as though it were the first time she had said, "Warren and I" in the same sentence. Her discomfort — which was either at having to deliver this news, or at having to admit to having had sex with Warren — was palpable. He could let her go on, uncomfortably so, or he could join the kids in the car, who were already fighting over who got the front seat.

*Decided?*

*Right. I mean, we haven't decided. But I am keeping her. I mean it. I mean, I think it is a her.* And Kate pressed one hand to her lower belly. We always talked about having more kids. *I'm just sorry we didn't keep Duncan's cradle*, she confided, as though he were her mother, or another baby-friend.

*Got it. Right. It was a nice cradle.*

*Not just nice*, she said, smiling — in what he would have taken to be flirtatious, or at least, loving, had he not just heard of her impregnation by the pale, potato-esque Warrenator. *You made it. It was gorgeous. Everyone used to call it the Cradle of Christ, remember? Those carvings!*

*Yeah. I remember. Well. Good luck. You take care of — well, of yourself.* He hastened to turn away, to face the car, the oaks, anything that wasn't her.

*See you*, she said. *Thanks for taking this so well. You've really — I guess — begun to blossom lately*, she said. *I wish it had been like this before. It means a lot to me.*

*Don't mention it.* Sam walked to the car, fluttering a goodbye just as he heard her shut the screen door. Kids, he said, pulling the shoulder strap down to arch across his body — his virile, less-lumpy-than-Warren body, looking at their listless sweaty faces in the back seat. *Hey kids! Anyone want to go to Disneyland?*

★

He hadn't stopped seeing Andrea, exactly. They had stopped seeing each other after one weird conversation, in which she "bore her soul" to him, telling him that she realized he really ought to know something important about her, this one detail she had neglected. He leaned in, waiting to hear about a marriage overseas in Guinea or a conversion to Mormonism when she said, *Look, Sam. I like you. I like you a lot. You're kind of hot, even if you are a little older. But I'm not a monogamist. In fact, I don't even think monogamy really exists, you know? So I see other people. It's who I am. But I don't want to be ...* and she faltered here a bit, looking for the right words on the wind. *A wife, wife substitute. I'm not into it. I'm sure you understand.* And he had smelled this, right, in his lizard brain, while at her back-pad, the sense that others had been here before him and others would no doubt christen it since? *I prefer,* she said, looking at him with what he might have, in his younger, more inept years, mistaken for love, but now wholly saw for what it was, which was pity — *loose arrangements. It's for Dizzy's sake, really,* she said, watching as Dizzy spun around and around in a circle, true to his name, a tiny beige helicopter, his hair pointed at magnetic north, turning mindlessly around while gazing up at the sky. *I want him to — you know — be able to really love his dad in his own right, without the confines of my relationships being a part of his construct of what it is to grow up. You know?*

He nodded. The explanation was strangely academic, as though she had borrowed it from a course she was taking, Hegemony and Human Events 101 or Phil 305: Philosophy of Polygamy. *I just don't want him feeling, you know, confused.*

*I don't want to — you know — sound like I am trying to talk you out of this,* he edged forward. *But isn't having a different man around all the time confusing for him?*

*The only man in Dizzy's life*, she said, buckling her purse, getting ready to make a getaway, *should really be his father. You know, Freud and all. I don't want him feeling he has to compete with another particular male. His construct of what it is to be a man — it really should be, you know, based on his own father, not my facsimile of one. That would be so — you know — conventionally Oedipal. Or maybe Antigonal. I'm not sure.* She sighed, stood up, signaling to him that the conversation was over. *But, I hope you'll come hear us play next week at Frankie's?* He nodded, dimly aware that he had absolutely no plans for the day — for the weekend, really — beyond this trip to the park with her and Dizzy, who had finally collapsed in a pile of leaves, which he was using to bury himself. *I'm alive! I'm alive!* he sang as the leaves rained down on him. His own kids, once again, were with Kate, who was sitting patiently with them while Denise finished her science report on asteroids and Duncan made them Shake and Bake chicken. He had no plans. The entirety of his plan had been to see Andrea with the prospect of Dizzy-less sex hanging in the horizon. Projects were thin. Employment — the thing that had until now separated him from many of The Quarry's residents — was irregular, and his free time, once scarce, was now abundant, like game in the wilds without a predator in sight.

★

Anita was the third woman he dated. She was the manager of the local organic coop, and she smelled like a combination of seitan and tea tree oil, neither of which were particularly sexy to Sam. But she was a boy's girl, she loved talking tile and molding; she was remodeling her house on her own, and had called Sam to come over and give her a bid on reseating her toilet, which, given her stature — petite, bordering on miniature — was impossible to do alone. He was impressed by her command of sealants and grout. Her results looked more artistic than professional; his trained eye pained at the fact that no level had been used to seat the counters and they were a bit askew.

*I don't want you to think that just because you're having to work on my toilet, I think of you as the plumber*, she said. Her tool belt sagged appreciably below her small waist.

*I don't have to just be the plumber*, he said. It sounded porny and weird and he looked down at the seating to avert his eyes from her. But when he handed her a receipt for his parts and labor, she slipped him a card for 5% off his next organic smoothie purchase. Her cell number, with her name and a tiny heart, were on the back. He waited one and a half days — embroiled in fantasies of fucking her on her pretty, albeit tilted tiled floor — and called to ask her to dinner on Saturday night.

*I know this doesn't sound like a reason*, she said. *But it's true. And it doesn't mean I don't want to see you. It's just that I'm going to a psychic faire this weekend. So I'm kind of busy.*

*A psychic faire?*

*You know, tarot. Past-life regression. Numerology. You know? The whole co-op usually goes, practically, but this year the annual Vegan Society meeting conflicts.* He didn't know. His idea of a past life was one in which Kate was still lovingly preparing baked macaroni and cheese with those tiny sausages for him and rolling up his jeans to slide her hand up his leg.

*Want company?* he asked, tentatively, expecting Anita to say no. Instead, she said, *really, really? I'd love to take you with me. Everyone will love your energy.* He didn't know what that meant. It made him sound more like a Golden Retriever than a man. But that was how he found himself having his rutted, blistered palms read in a green tent by a woman whose name was Madame Lapin.

*Hold out your hands,* she told him, and he did, aware of how blistered they were, how thick, how unattractive. Madame Lapin looked for a few moments, saying nothing. Finally, she sighed. *I see a whirlwind.* He was sitting with Anita, who was holding his other hand. Her cheek was painted with a metallic butterfly and she was wearing what could be described as fairy wings. She had tucked her other hand down the edge of his pants, right above his ass, and he was both titillated and annoyed — she was proving to be less attractive by the minute, all high-pitched squeals and positive affirmations. *You're amazing. Everyone loves you.* And the worst one, which she said when he had undressed in front of her last night for the first time, *You're such a big boy, aren't you?* He had big plans, it was true, and they had catapulted radically since last night, from bathroom-floor fantasy to not seeing her again after the Faire ended.

*A whirlwind?*

*A whirlwind. Like, Job. Except you are not like Job. Job accepts his fate. You don't.*

*I don't?*

*No. But you'll see. Your life, as you know it, is toppling. Like Job's. Also like Gomorrah.*

*The city? As in, Sodom and?*

*He's smart for such a square-handed man,* Madame Lapin said, as an aside, to Anita, who was listening intently.

*He's amazing,* Anita said for the seventh time that day.

*Yes,* said Madame Lapin, closing his fingers back into his hand to indicate she had seen all she needed. *Like Sodom and. Go in peace, John Walton,* she said, winking not once but twice, tucking the ten bucks he'd paid for her wisdom into the corner of her bra.

★

The months wheeled by. The baby grew inside his former wife in the same manner as their babies had grown and shaped her; each time he saw her, he was amazed by the fact that she had done this with someone else. It was like returning to a home he had built or remodeled to find it had been dismantled entirely, its insides gutted, each little screw he had screwed tenderly and with love unscrewed and rubbed into the dust. Warren moved in, bringing with him his Ford Focus, which was exactly the kind of car Sam had hoped he would have, square and cheap. Sam had stopped dating anyone, or they had stopped dating him. His apartment had gone to shambles, paperwork in the bathroom, tools in the living room; Denise stubbed her toe on one of his boxes and swore for the first time, screaming at the metal. *Fucking Asshole!!* The kids came and left The Quarry like a pair of migrating geese, winter, summer, winter, summer, the weekends the seasons, the weekdays a purgatory of loneliness, Fridays at One for the Road with Gus. He worked, he didn't work, it was all the same. The kids seemed nonplussed at the arrival of the baby. Duncan in particular pretended it wasn't happening, and Denise vacillated between a motherly nurturance and horror.

*Warren moved in*, she whined at him. He's so gross.

*I know, sweetie,* he said, without thinking. She leaned against him.

*He farts weird*, she said. *And then pretends he didn't.*

Sam kept quiet. If he interfered, he risked her silence.

*And he wants to name the baby Mitchell if it is a boy.*

*Mitchell? Why on earth Mitchell?*

*Dad*, she said, *how should I know why? Do I look like God? Because he's a jerk!*

*Also, he uses my crayons*, chirped Duncan. *Except the ochre one. Nobody likes that color.*

*Why?*

*To color!* Duncan said, as though Sam were lacking in intellectual faculties.

*Right*, he said. Why was a grown accountant coloring in his free time? Kate clearly was out of her mind. The conversation dwindled, and the car mysteriously ended up in front of the kids' favorite ice creamery. *Anyone for Blueberry Cheesecake?* he asked, but didn't have to, as they left the car before he had finished parking.

★

The baby arrived in August, entering the world two weeks early and claiming his destiny as the unfortunately-named Mitchell. He was colicky, according to Denise, due to his *premature digestive tract*, words she had no doubt absorbed from her mother. Both Denise and Duncan had been colicky, so this detail pleased him very much. It meant that, as he had suspected even then, Kate was the colicky one, and had passed on her sensitivity, rather than the other way around. Duncan took to the infant with a magical, inbred prowess; he was the self-appointed baby-sitter and pinch-hitter for the kid, taking him out in a small umbrella stroller to scream his little tiny screams at the wide neighborhood where they once walked their own kids. Still — with the late nights the baby put in, and school beginning — the kids ended up at his apartment more often than they used to. They were used children, not spanking new like Mitchell, and it was time to pass them on. So now they spent weekdays at his place and weekends with Kate and Warren and the baby.

*That little shit*, Denise said, when she got in the car. *He's so cute, but he kept me up all night. It's more like having a cousin. He isn't one of us.*

*He's half us*, said Duncan, from the back seat.

*Half you, maybe. He's so* — *Warren. It's like even though he is a little shit right now and he poops up his own back, he'll be an accountant or something. I don't know if he is trainable to be like us.*

*And guess what?* Duncan said, craning himself so he was inched out of his seatbelt, just a breath away from Sam's face. *Warren and Mom are going to knock out a couple of walls for the baby's room. Warren says he doesn't like the way the windows are situated, either.* It was unlike Duncan to include a word such as "situated" in his daily vocabulary. It sounded much more like accountant-speak. It made Sam a little queasy; he had to open his window to pick up a draft.

*Yeah?*

*Yeah, they said they're gonna have some work done on the house while they're on their honeymoon. But Warren is paying for it, Daddy, so don't worry.*

*Is that right?*

*Daddy*, said Denise. *Are you upset?*

*No, sweetie. Maybe a little. I built that house, you know. So it is a little hard to hear.*

*We know*, they chanted from the back seat.

★

*Further back, I think* she whispered, watching as he shifted a box to the right with a broom handle, shards of orange cat hairs drifting from the ticking as he forced one box over. *Look behind that one.* He torqued the broom for leverage and a Halloween pumpkin careened out of the rafters and landed a few feet from her sandals, pieces of Double-Bubble hardened by time scattering behind them. His heart was racing; even though Warren and Kate were in Hawaii with the baby, claiming their honeymoon at last, he felt the sense of being a child on the verge of getting caught.

*I don't see anything, honey*, he said, continuing to poke about. *You're pretty sure?*

*Daddy. Yes.*

He stood on the top rung of the ladder and pushed aside another box. Behind it was a mesh bag, the single eye of an ancient Snoopy gazing its forlorn threaded stare at them. She screamed, her arms lifting up as he lassoed the sack of animals down from the rafters. Denise continued to happy-cry, plunging her hand into the pillowcase full of the long-lost cadre of stuffed friends. The arrival of the baby, the changing of residences, and the beginning of another school year had put Denise in a rough spot, and the comforts of the past — some appearing to be regressive — seemed critical to her well being. He climbed down, dusted his hands on his jeans, folded the ladder and leaned it back against the wall.

*Sweetie, we should really go. It's a little —* he hesitated, uncertain of what to say next. It wasn't illegal, exactly, to bring his daughter to her own house to get the one set of items he knew she would miss if it was gone.

But it probably was illegal, though he doubted at this point that his undercover mission to lift a few Snoopies from her rafters would be the centrifuge of friction. *Strange. Strange to be here.*

*Yeah,* she said. *I mean, you built this house. It really is more like yours than Mom's. And it sure ain't Warren's. It's so unfair.*

*Honey, please don't say "ain't." It's trashy.*

*Dad, you're trashy.*

He checked his pockets, climbed down from the ladder, and walked out to the car with her. Duncan was on the grass — the deep green fescue he'd planted three years ago himself, long and soft. The kids got into the back seat. Sam climbed in, strapped the seat belt, looked up the slight hill at the house — so perfect, so beautifully built, that for the first time he really saw it as it was, his life work.

*Shoot, I forgot something in the garage. You two wait here.*

*Dad!! We're hungry!*

*Just one second. Wait here. I'll be back in two shakes.* And he ran back to the garage. He grabbed a couple small boxes of photos from the file cabinet, and the Snoopy sleeping bag he knew Denise loved, a few other well-loved elementals of their baby lives. Then he locked up the house and drove the kids to Elmo's Pizzeria for orange soda and deep-dish pepperoni, their very favorite.

★

The phone in his pocket kept buzzing, buzzing. It was Gus, then Gus again, then again. He considered not answering it — he was trying, after all, not to model behavior that would enable his children in future years — but after the fifth call, he handed the kids a pocketful of quarters for the video games and picked up. *Sorry! Was ordering some pizza for the kids! What's up, man?*

*Kate's house. I mean, your old house. It's on fire. Did you —*

*What? Why, that's terrible. I — wow. I wonder if I ought to call her. They're in Hawaii. Must have left something on —*

*I think the Fire Department probably did, man. This is crazy, though. You gonna be okay? The kids with you?*

*Yeah. I'll talk to them. Wow, man. Thanks for the call. See you next week, yep?*

*Right. Hang in there, man. I know how much the place meant to you.*

*Yeah. Let's hope The Warrenator paid the fire premium this year, ha.*

*I sure hope so, man. Geez. What a mess. Hey, take it easy.*

*You, too.*

★

The question before the jury had not really been whether or not Sam had done anything. That he had entered the house unlawfully — his house, the one he built with his own two hands, *unlawfully?* — was certain. But what remained in contest had to do with the degree of planning before doing so. *Premeditation, as we have discussed throughout this trial, is the specific intent to commit a crime for some period of time, however short, before the actual crime is committed,* began his lawyer, in what would turn into the most artfully melancholic closing remarks. *And if you sub-tract the word, "crime," and look at the idea of intent, it fits well with so many other institutions — marriage, for one. Nobody wakes up married. You know that there are going to be these occurrences — a ceremony of sorts, a cake, per-haps, a ring, a set of vows. They are exchanged with meaning, and intention, and hopefully, with delight. Marriage does not just happen to couples participating in its ancient rite; it is premeditated, is it not? Like divorce, yes? Some of you, fellow citizens,* and here he gestured at the jury, *are all too likely acquainted with divorce, with the failure of such a large project as a relationship. It doesn't happen overnight, am I right, members of the jury? It is an incubation period, of happiness and unhappiness, nights crying alone, an epiphany, perhaps, of oneself as better off alone, or a moment of seduction. You have heard testimonies and seen photographs. But are we talking about the destruction of property, or a premeditated crime? This is what you must decide.* Sam sat quietly, his face burning. Had he pre-plotted the clipping of one wire and the connection of another, so that when the lights came on as per their timers at the correct hour of the day for the absent honeymooners, a small pop — one could say, a fragmentary explosion — would result? How long before said action did he think about it? An hour? A day? Months? He really wasn't sure.

Most of those who were called to testify — both on his behalf, and against him — felt compelled to discuss their level of surprise, as though this were part of the equation. The trial became a little like the old show, "This Is Your Life," with each guest letting the audience know what they had expected of Sam from the moment they had met him, as though the degree of their surprise were directly linked, or not, to his guilt. Gus was surprised. *I — I think it's hard*, he had said tearfully, *for us to fully know how lonely he was. I mean, he was living in this place called The Quarry. Have you seen that place? It was about to be condemned. Full of hippies and hipsters. He didn't fit in, man. He was alone. And he'd built that house himself. I never did think it was right that she* — and he gestured in the general direction of Kate, who held a wiggling little Mitchell on her lap to keep him from toddling about the courtroom — *kept the house.* When Kate was called to the stand, she said she was surprised at first, because Sam had been so kind and accepting of her new marriage. But she did say, *He seemed to be changing, though. Different. At first I thought it was a good thing. But now when I look back*, and here she looked at the jury, tearfully, woefully, *I think he just finally snapped.* She said, a bit wistfully, Sam thought, *He is a brilliant contractor, really. He would have known exactly what to do.*

For Sam, the surprise wasn't in the small electrical malfunctions that had occurred in his former residence, the little sparks, the waves of heat that rippled through the walls as he and the children drove down the hill to Elmo's, singing to *Don't Stop Believing* with the windows of the car wide open to the evening air that was just beginning to cool. Nor was it in the fantastic flame he knew would burst out from inside the roof, the insulation serving as a fantastical conductor; spinning its pink stuffed bits like cotton candy into the singed grass. It wasn't in the faces of his former neighbors, who by their own accounts stood outside to watch the spectacle, their cheeks rosy with the heat. It wasn't in the frantic sound of Kate's voice on the phone, when she called him from her Hawaiian retreat, an hour or so before the cops arrived at the Quarry, inadvertently sending a fleet of stoners to hide in the UFO site — *the police called me, Sam, what the fuck? Did you do this? Did you burn down our house?* And, by *our,* he knew she meant not *his* house, but the house that belonged to her and Warren, and he got her to calm down enough to tell her that Denise and Duncan were fine, just fine, they were down in the Mikvah right this minute, floating the little sailboats he had bought them at Sea World last weekend. The surprise was in the moments just before everything happened — before he retrieved the stuffed bears, the beany babies, the bedraggled kitty Duncan carted around for years named July, the matted doll Denise had named, improbably, Russia Mafia, two words she must have overheard on the radio and found beautiful — when he felt a sharp sense of clarity, of order. His place in the world — long obscured by events he could not control — had become clear. He no longer felt awkward or uncertain. When he pulled away for the last time from the woodsy edges of the suburban development Kate had chosen for their tiny green square stamp of land, small enough that, from an aerial view a few thousand feet above, he imagined it to resemble a grave, he had felt a sense of both watching his life and living it in the exact same moment, a moment he had created alone, with his own two realistic hands, and that, once in motion, he would never have to return to.

## A Note on the Type

The body text in this issue is set in Bembo, an old-style serif typeface produced by Monotype in 1928. The face is based on a type design by Francesco Griffo in 1495 for a book by Pietro Bembo.


## Longship Press

Longship Press is an independent, small-press publisher of literature, memoir, educational materials, and art. *Nostos*, the literary journal published by Longship Press, seeks poetry, short fiction, and art throughout the year for its two editions each year. Concepts for book publication may be submitted at any time. Please contact the Editor at

info@longshippress.com